SACRAMENTO PUBLIC LIBRARY
828 "I" Street
Sacramento, CA 95814
7/11

D0118960

HOW PEOPLE LIVED

DK

London, New York,
Melbourne, Munich, and Delhi

Senior editor Shaila Brown
Senior art editor Sheila Collins
Designer Katie Knutton

Managing editor Linda Esposito
Managing art editor Jim Green
Category publisher Laura Buller

Picture researchers Karen VanRoss and Ria Jones
DK picture library Claire Bowers

Senior production controller Angela Graef
Production editor Marc Staples

Jacket designer Laura Brim
Jacket editor Matilda Gollen
Senior development editor Jayne Miller
Development designer Laura Brim
Design development manager Sophia M. Tampakopoulos Turner

Consultant John Haywood

First published in the United States in 2011 by DK Publishing
375 Hudson Street, New York, New York 10014

Copyright © 2011 Dorling Kindersley Limited

11 12 13 14 15 10 9 8 7 6 5 4 3 2 1
001–180647–05/11

All rights reserved under International and Pan-American Copyright Conventions.
No part of this publication may be reproduced, stored in a retrieval system,
or transmitted in any form or by any means, electronic, mechanical, photocopying,
recording, or otherwise, without the prior written permission of the copyright owner.
Published in Great Britain by Dorling Kindersley Limited.

DK books are available at special discounts when purchased in bulk for sales promotions,
premiums, fundraising, or educational use. For details, contact: DK Publishing Special Markets,
375 Hudson Street, New York, New York 10014, SpecialSales@dk.com

A catalog record for this book
is available from the Library of Congress.

ISBN: 978-0-7566-8275-0

Hi-res workflow proofed by MDP, UK
Printed by Star Standard Industries Pte, Singapore

Discover more at
www.dk.com

HOW PEOPLE LIVED

WRITTEN BY JIM PIPE

ILLUSTRATIONS BY ZACK McLAUGHLIN

CONTENTS

THE STORY BEGINS . . .

This book gives a snapshot of how people have lived through the ages—from cave dwellers wading through tide pools for food to today's high-tech societies that can send people into space or microwave a meal in seconds. In the early days, humans were on the move, hunting animals and gathering wild fruits, nuts, and roots. But about 10,000 years ago, they discovered a new way of living: farming. Now more people could stay in one place and build towns. There was spare food to support craftspeople making pots, jewelry, and shiny stone mirrors. Working together, the ancient Egyptians built pyramids and seagoing ships, while the ancient Romans enjoyed hot, steamy baths and gladiator fights (when they weren't conquering the world). On the other side of the globe, the Maya constructed towering temples.

Back in Europe, the fall of the Roman Empire led to the gloomy Dark Ages. Most people were too busy fighting each other (or hiding from the Vikings) to think of new inventions. Not so in medieval China, where business boomed and bright ideas such as gunpowder, the compass, and paper money showed the rest of the world the way forward. Although life was speeding up in Europe, the vast majority of people still lived in the country, where life followed the changing seasons. Half a world away, salt and gold traders traveled hundreds of miles to do business in the African town of Timbuktu. Here, Muslim scholars studied in great universities, whose fame reached even inside the walls of the Topkapi Palace in Istanbul, home to the Ottoman sultan and his many wives.

By the 18th century, the world was really on the move. European sailors had traveled the globe, bringing back coffee, sugar, and tea. In the drawing rooms of European cities such as Vienna, writers and thinkers chatted endlessly about science and freedom before taking a spin in the ballroom. Not everyone wanted change. On the Pacific coast of Canada, people still lived by fishing and gathering wild berries and shellfish—a world away from the smoking factories and steam trains of industrial England. New inventions came fast and furious—telephones, electric lights, and planes—and by the 1950s, whole towns in the United States were built around the car. A generation later, ox-drawn carts were still a common sight on the streets of India, but even there, life was about to speed up. Today, the entire population of the Roman Empire could fit in a single city, Tokyo. Who knows—your grandchildren may end up living on the moon or Mars!

As you fly around the world in the following pages, keep an eye out for the caveman who left Pinnacle Point around 160,000 years ago for a time-traveling adventure. Turn to pages 72–73 to see if you spotted him, and while you're there, test your knowledge of history by solving some mind-boggling riddles.

CAVE DWELLERS

Around 160,000 years ago, a group of early humans are living in the caves of Pinnacle Point on the southern coast of South Africa. While some members of the group hunt for wildlife or dig for edible roots and bulbs on the heathland above, others search for mussels and limpets on the rocks below. Their tools are made of stone and bone, their clothes from animal skins. They have learned to live and work together. If they don't, they probably won't survive!

Modern humans first appear around 200,000 years ago. Living on the grasslands of Africa, they hunt and scavenge during the day, avoiding big predators such as lions that hunt at night. Then, around 195,000 years ago, things get a lot tougher. The Earth enters a great Ice Age that lasts for about 70,000 years. The grasslands become cold and dry, killing many of the plants that early humans rely on for food. Pinnacle Point is one of just a few places where survival is possible. Although it's a stormy coastline, the caves offer great protection against the wind and rain, and the sea provides food in the form of shellfish, seals, and other marine life. The survivors live in small bands of up to 30 members. They use fire to keep themselves warm, to cook, and to ward off predators. By watching the moon, they may even be able to predict when the tide is low—the best time to forage for food in the tide pools. They carefully fashion tools and weapons by chipping away at stones until they have a sharp edge. Life is hard, but there is time for family life, play, and laughter.

LIFE AT PINNACLE POINT

Although they lived more than 160,000 years ago, the early humans who inhabited Pinnacle Point looked—and thought—just like people today. In fact, every person alive today is probably descended from a small group of survivors who made it through the great Ice Age. The harsh conditions forced our ancestors to think of new ways to live, hunt, and communicate. They created new tools and got in touch with their artistic side, making paint from red rocks.

BELONGING

Just like people today, early humans probably used clothing, jewelry, hairstyles, and makeup to show they belonged to a particular group.

STONE-AGE LIVING

More than a million years ago, early humans were already using fire at Swartkrans in South Africa, where around 270 bones were apparently burned over campfires. So it's very likely fire was used at Pinnacle Point for cooking and heating.

Jewelry was made from readily available materials, such as shells, teeth, and bone

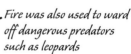

Red ocher was mixed with water to make body paint or color walls and objects

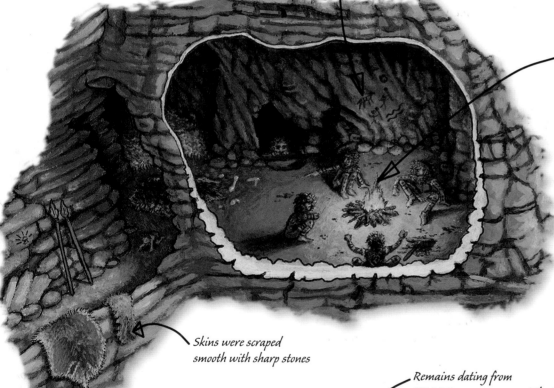

Fire was also used to ward off dangerous predators such as leopards

Skins were scraped smooth with sharp stones

Remains dating from 110,000 years ago suggest that seashells were also collected because they were beautiful

SEAFOOD PLATTER

The inhabitants of Pinnacle Point feasted on giant periwinkles, sea snails, brown mussels, limpets, and even the barnacles from whales. They probably waited for low tide to collect such morsels, since there was less chance of being knocked off their feet by an incoming wave.

Map

Swartkrans •

SOUTH AFRICA Sibudu Cave •

• Diepkloof

Pinnacle Point • • Klasies River Mouth
Blombos Cave

SOUTH AFRICA

Many important Middle Stone Age sites are found in South Africa, including Blombos Cave, Klasies River Mouth, and Diepkloof (these date from 75,000 to 55,000 years ago). Remarkably advanced tools have been found here, such as the first bone tools, special scrapers for cleaning animal hides, and tiny stone flakes used to turn spears into harpoons for catching fish.

HEAT-TREATED ROCKS

Archeologists have found large pieces of hard rock embedded in ash, such as the ones shown above. They believe the people at Pinnacle Point roasted rocks in a fire pit, so they were easier to flake into sharp weapons. This process requires several careful steps, which may suggest that these early humans were using language to pass on instructions.

CUTTING-EDGE TECHNOLOGY

Some of the most common artifacts found at Pinnacle Point are tiny flakes of stone known as bladelets. They're so small they must have been set in a handle, making an advanced tool with spikes, such as a harpoon for catching fish.

SEWING KIT

Bone needles have been found at another South African site, Sibudu Cave, suggesting that Middle Stone Age people could have made clothes around 60,000 years ago.

FOOD FOR THOUGHT

Organic material rarely survives more than a few thousand years, so it's difficult to know exactly what people ate. But, since food was scarce, it's likely that every available source was used, from robbing honey from bees' nests to stealing birds' eggs. The region around Pinnacle Point is also home to a group of plants called fynbos. These have very nutritious underground bulbs and tubers, and they would have been easily uprooted by an early human forager armed with a digging stick.

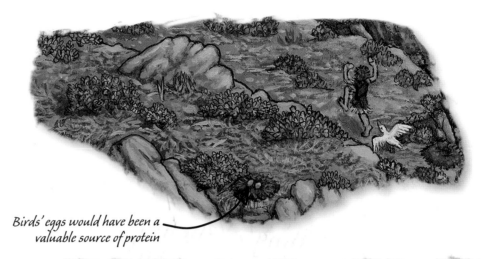

Birds' eggs would have been a valuable source of protein

RED OCHER

In Blombos Cave on the southern coast of South Africa, archeologists unearthed this piece of red ocher with geometric patterns scratched onto it. Around 75,000 years old, it is one of the world's oldest pieces of art.

Hunters learned to stand downwind of prey to avoid being detected

ON THE HUNT

The hunters at Pinnacle Point probably didn't have bows and arrows, but they were armed with axes and spears made from sharpened stones attached to wooden handles. These would have shattered if thrown, so the spears were probably used for thrusting at prey such as gazelles or beached whales.

EARLY FARMERS

It's 6000 BCE. Although this is still the Stone Age, humans have learned to grow crops and breed animals. A roving trader looks up in awe at the human-made mountain before him. This is the town of Çatal Hüyük, home to around 5,000 people—and the most crowded place on Earth. His feet ache from the long journey and his stomach groans with hunger. But the trip has been worth it. The local farmers are only too happy to swap food and stone tools for the brightly colored shells in his hand.

People here in southwest Asia have learned a new trick—if they store food, they no longer have to move every year to feed their families. In fact, the prosperous farmers living in Çatal Hüyük produce so much food they can trade what they don't need with their neighbors. They have built permanent homes from brick, and slowly their settlement has grown from a few houses into a bustling town filled with stone workers, weavers, and potters. People travel from far afield to trade shells from the Red Sea or flint from Syria. They also come to barter for obsidian, a highly prized rock from an extinct volcano nearby that is used to make razor-sharp tools. On the rooftops, animal pelts used for clothing are left to dry in the hot sun. Below the town walls, some farmers are busy harvesting the crops, while others make bricks from mud. There are no public buildings, but all the houses look very similar. Above the hubbub, there is the sound of singing and wailing. There are no priests in this town, but people come together in household shrines to worship their gods and pray for the souls of dead relatives. For Çatal Hüyük is a home for both the living and the dead.

THE FIRST TOWNS

Around 9,000 years old, Çatal Hüyük is one of the oldest Stone Age towns ever found. It's also one of the best preserved. There are no written records, but many walls decorated with paintings survive, along with the remains of objects such as bone tools, clothing, wooden bowls, and woven mats.

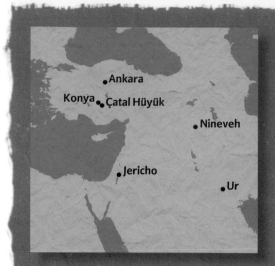

There were no streets or alleys, so people got around by walking up ladders and across roofs

Houses were entered through hatches in the roofs

ANCIENT SOUTHWEST ASIA

Most of the world's first towns, such as Nineveh, Ur, and Jericho, were found in southwest Asia. Çatal Hüyük, near Konya in modern Turkey, was one of the biggest towns. Why? It was built next to the River Carsamba in the middle of a fertile plain—a perfect spot for farming, breeding animals, and hunting wildlife.

TUMBLEDOWN TOWN

Çatal Hüyük was a maze of hundreds of tightly packed mud-brick houses. After about 80 years, the mud in the walls began to crumble. The family inside knocked the old house down and built a new one on top using the same timbers. This went on for almost 2,000 years, by which time the whole town sat on a 65 ft (20 m) high mound called a tell. Since the outer walls had no windows or doors, Çatal Hüyük was like a fortress.

ARTFUL HUNTERS

Several wall paintings in Çatal Hüyük show running men with leopard skins tied around their waists, so there were probably leopards living nearby as well as wild boars, foxes, and deer. In one wall painting, a hunter carries a curved stick, possibly a bow.

A LAND OF PLENTY

The people of Çatal Hüyük were among the first to keep animals such as chickens, ducks, cattle, deer, and donkeys. Goats were bred for milk and meat and kept in pens between the houses. Outside the city, farmers grew wheat and barley as well as peas, nuts, seeds, and berries (used to make berry wine), while almonds and fruit were picked from wild trees. Crops were harvested using tools made of obsidian, a glassy volcanic stone that holds a sharp cutting edge.

MOTHER GODDESS

Just 8 in (20 cm) tall, this statuette of a pregnant Mother Goddess was found in Çatal Hüyük. Made from clay and seated on a throne, the leopards on either side show her power.

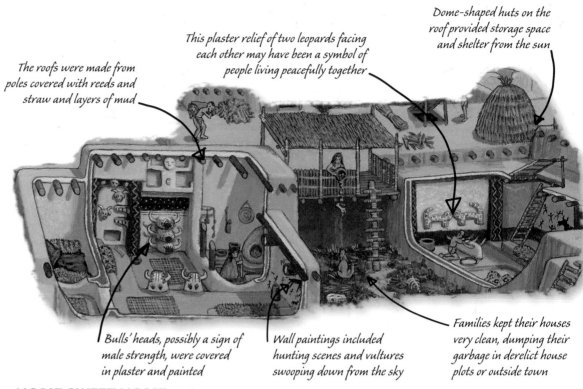

The roofs were made from poles covered with reeds and straw and layers of mud

This plaster relief of two leopards facing each other may have been a symbol of people living peacefully together

Dome-shaped huts on the roof provided storage space and shelter from the sun

Bulls' heads, possibly a sign of male strength, were covered in plaster and painted

Wall paintings included hunting scenes and vultures swooping down from the sky

Families kept their houses very clean, dumping their garbage in derelict house plots or outside town

HOME SWEET HOME

A typical house in Çatal Hüyük had a main room with two side rooms for storage. Without windows, it was dark and stuffy, so in warm, dry weather many daily tasks were performed on the rooftops, which were the town's streets and plazas. In winter, houses were heated by a stove, while ovens shaped like horseshoes were used for baking. There was no furniture. People ate and slept on benches made from raised banks of earth and covered in mats, and stored their belongings in niches built into the walls.

There were religious items or shrines in most houses—the same room was used for everyday tasks as well as acts of worship

Dead relatives were buried in pits under the floor

To make bricks, mud and straw were mixed by stomping on them

The mixture was placed in a mold and allowed to dry

BURIED BONES

It might seem spooky today, but the people of Çatal Hüyük buried their dead within the town. After death, most corpses were left in the open so vultures could pick the bones clean. The skeletons were then wrapped in cloth while the skulls were plastered and painted red to look like faces. Finally, the whole skeletons were buried with gifts—women were often buried with necklaces and makeup kits including shells filled with red ocher, while men were buried with flint daggers.

DOING THEIR JOBS

There were all kinds of jobs in Çatal Hüyük, since more and more people lived by making goods and trading them for food. Down by the river, mud was shaped into bricks using a simple wooden mold and left to bake in the sun. In the town, craftspeople flaked and polished stone axes and mirrors, made tools, and wove baskets and mats. They also painted clay pots and crafted beautiful copper earrings and necklaces made from beads and boar tusks.

EGYPTIAN TEMPLE

Ancient Egypt is a rich and prosperous land. Once a year, the mighty Nile River floods, leaving behind a rich black mud that's excellent for growing crops. To the Egyptians, living in the middle of a desert, this is a magical event. To give thanks to the gods, they build magnificent temples for them to live in. Only priests and priestesses may enter the temple, while townspeople watch in wonder as sacred statues of the gods are brought into the interior, hidden from view in shining caskets of gold.

Our scene is set in the New Kingdom (1570–1070 BCE). The Great Pyramids are already a thousand years old, but life has hardly changed in that time. Year after year, the Nile keeps on giving; it's a source of fresh fish as well as fresh water. The great river is also Egypt's highway. Large ships transport heavy cargoes from one part of the kingdom to another, such as stones for building, jars filled with grain, or teams of officials working for the Egyptian king, the pharaoh. The Egyptians know about wheels, but on land the heavy lifting is done with sleds and donkeys. Most villagers work in the fields. It's hard working in the hot sun, whether they're herding cattle and ducks, plowing the soil with a team of oxen, or reaping barley and wheat with a sickle. Town life revolves around the temple, which organizes the collection and storage of grain in dome-shaped granaries. The temple also has its own bakeries, breweries, and schools for scribes. All in all, most Egyptians enjoy life so much they want it to go on even after they die. Teams of priests turn their bodies into mummies so they are preserved forever. Amazing tombs are built for the dead to live in, and kings are buried with fabulous treasures to enjoy after death.

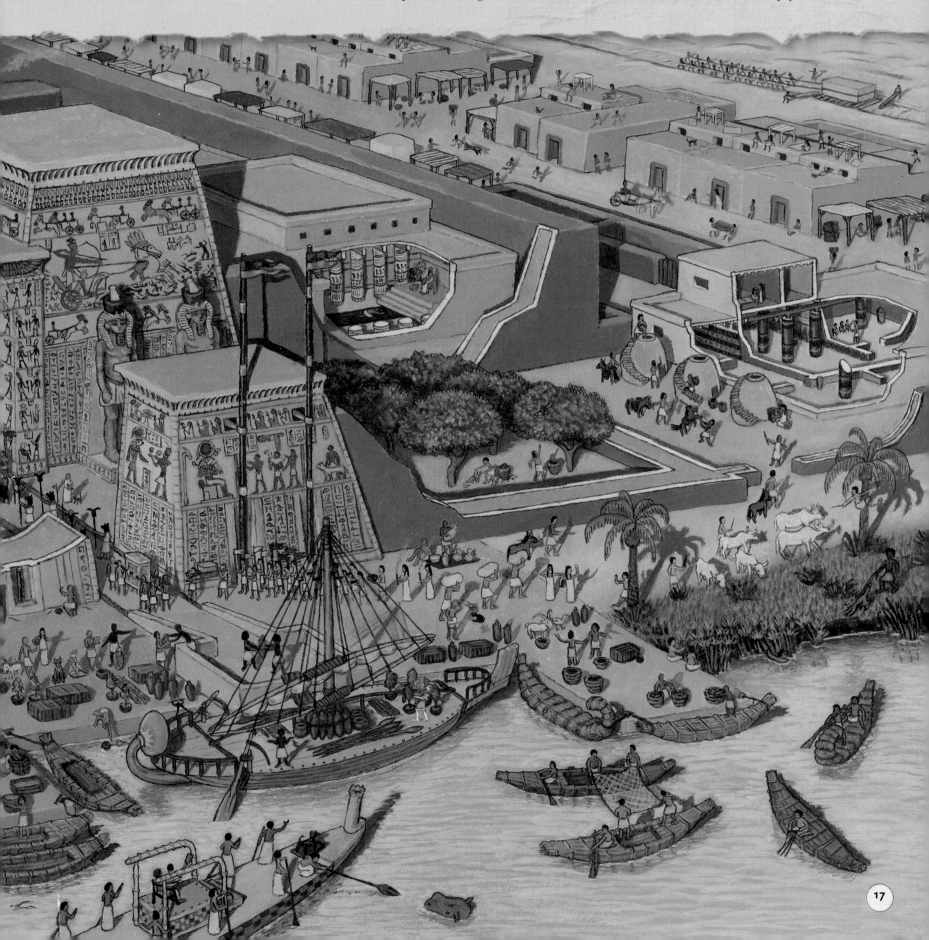

LIFE BY THE NILE

Ancient Egypt has always amazed people with its pyramids, hidden tombs, and golden treasures. But what were Egyptians really like? We've learned a lot from objects and paintings found in tombs. In their writings, they come across as happy people who loved life. But few Egyptians lived past 40, so they also spent a lot of energy and money planning for death. By preserving their dead bodies as mummies, they hoped to be born again in the next world.

Farmers used a device called a shaduf to lift water so they could irrigate their fields

EGYPTIAN EMPIRE

The Nile runs all the way through ancient Egypt. Even so, the ancient kingdom was cut off from the world by deserts to the east and west, dangerous waterfalls and rapids to the south, and the swampy Nile delta to the north. Although rarely threatened by invaders, Egypt's pharaohs fought campaigns in Syria to the north and Nubia and Kush to the south.

IN THE FIELDS

Egyptian farmers raised sheep, ducks, geese, and goats, while the number of cattle they owned was a sign of wealth. Some kept bees for honey, used to sweeten food. They also grew crops such as onions, dates, grapes, figs, wheat, and barley. After the wheat was cut, cattle were driven across it to separate the grain from the husk. When the wheat was tossed into the air, the lighter husk was blown away and the grain was stored in baskets.

RELIGION AND MAGIC

During the flood season, farmers were roped into public-service jobs, such as repairing ditches or building a new temple. In return, it was the pharaoh's job to maintain order in the world by making sure that offerings were made to the gods in the temples. Religion was a very important part of daily life. People prayed at home to local gods and goddesses such as Bes, who protected families. Most Egyptians were also incredibly superstitious. They believed wearing a magic charm could prevent illness or bring good luck.

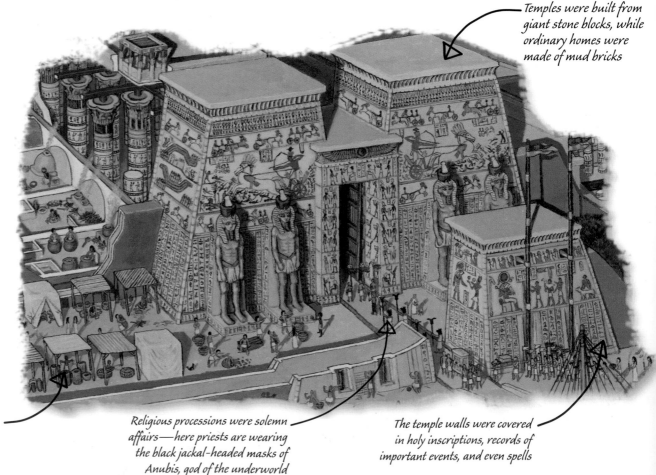

Temples were built from giant stone blocks, while ordinary homes were made of mud bricks

To avoid the heat of the midday sun, workers labored in the morning and late afternoon, with a long break in between

Religious processions were solemn affairs—here priests are wearing the black jackal-headed masks of Anubis, god of the underworld

The temple walls were covered in holy inscriptions, records of important events, and even spells

LONG DISTANCE DELIGHTS

The Egyptians were among the first to build long-distance sailing ships. Merchants traded grain and linen for gold from Nubia, copper from Cyprus, cedarwood from Lebanon, and spices and precious stones from the east. Exotic goods such as ivory, ostrich eggs, and leopard and lion skins came from the land of Punt in the south.

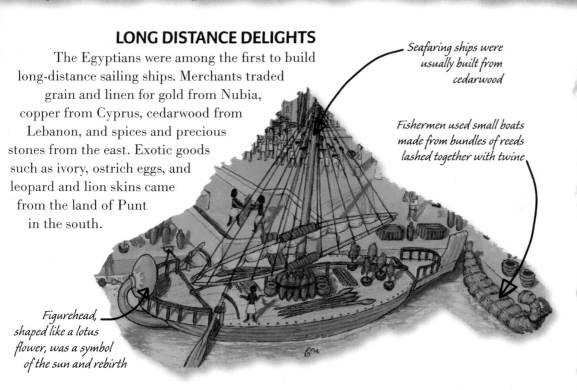

Seafaring ships were usually built from cedarwood

Fishermen used small boats made from bundles of reeds lashed together with twine

Figurehead, shaped like a lotus flower, was a symbol of the sun and rebirth

WRITING IN SYMBOLS

Ancient Egyptian writing is among the oldest in the world. Known as hieroglyphics, this sacred language was used mainly for inscriptions on the walls of temples and tombs. Each symbol had a meaning and a sound. For example, the symbol for crocodile also represented the sound "msh." Another, simpler script, called hieratic, was used for writing letters. But only a few Egyptians could read and write—most of them scribes. It took 12 years to learn all the hieroglyphics!

HUNTING AND FISHING

The ancient Egyptians were skilled hunters. They caught birds using spring-loaded nets and curved wooden throwing sticks (like the one in this scene from the tomb of Nebamun, a scribe). Nobles and pharaohs hunted big game in the desert, such as antelope and lions. Rich Egyptians were also among the first to enjoy fishing as a sport.

Hippos were hunted for their meat and because they trampled crops, but if a hippo capsized the canoe, even the best swimmers might not escape its crushing jaws

Donkeys, camels, and oxen were all used as beasts of burden

Some baboons were trained to pick figs and dates from trees, while others were used by the police to patrol the markets for thieves

HOLY CROCODILE!

The Egyptians lived in awe of the fearsome crocodiles and hippos that lived along the Nile. Like most animals, they were seen as living gods. Sobek, the crocodile god, was worshipped in the temple at Kom Ombo, where priests kept tame crocodiles as pets. Other sacred animals, such as cats, bulls, sheep, and baboons, were also kept in temples. When they died, they were turned into mummies.

ROMAN TOWN

Let's fast-forward to 130 CE. Smelly barbarians may enjoy living in the countryside, but any good Roman knows there's only one place to live—in town! Here even the poorest citizens can enjoy a trip to the baths, watch a thrilling gladiator show, or take pride in the fine buildings around the town square, or forum. If you're rich, life is even better. There are slaves to do your shopping, cooking, and washing. That leaves plenty of time to go to the theater, get involved in politics, or impress your friends with banquets of stuffed dormice and roast flamingos!

The Romans are great builders: Their towns are chock full of grand arches, soaring columns, and magnificent temples. They also love order. The paved streets are built in a neat grid centered around the forum, and a one-way system cuts down on traffic jams. There are police forces, aqueducts to bring fresh water from afar, and even giant toilets where customers can enjoy a leisurely chat with a group of friends. Despite all of this, Roman towns are noisy, crowded, and dirty. The forum echoes with the sound of businessmen striking deals, money changers jiggling coins in their hands to attract customers, and the jeers of spectators watching trials in the courtrooms. Nearby, a rich merchant haggles over the price of some slaves. The sound of rumbling wheels is so deafening that wagons and carts are banned from the streets at night so people can sleep. Meanwhile, the smell of animal waste and rotting food lying on the streets is overpowering. In larger towns, people often get sick or die from drinking water poisoned by sewage. Dark, narrow backstreets crawl with thieves and cutthroats. Maybe it's time to move back to the country!

BUILT TO LAST

Made of concrete, brick, and stone, Roman towns were built to last. Some buildings are still standing today. Roman documents and everyday objects also tell us how the Romans lived, and thanks to Christian monks who copied the original Latin manuscripts in the Middle Ages, we can still read the words of Roman writers more than 1,500 years after the Roman Empire ended.

ON THE STREET

As the Romans went about their everyday business, they passed through streets crowded with shops and markets selling goods from every corner of the empire. There were wine shops, bakers, barbers, shoemakers, blacksmiths, and florists. Shops opened out onto the street and sold goods from dawn to dusk. The Romans loved fast food—they could buy snacks and hot drinks from takeout restaurants called *thermopolia* or from vendors who carried trays on their heads.

ROMAN EMPIRE

At its height around 150 CE, it is estimated that 70 million people lived within the borders of the Roman Empire (shaded in brown). It was the largest empire the world had ever known, and was divided into provinces, each ruled by a Roman governor. Every time they conquered a new territory, the Romans built a network of roads linking it with Rome, the capital.

The floors above Roman shops were often divided into apartments—whole families lived in a single room

Graffiti was common— "Satura was here" and "Epaphra is a baldy!" were found on the walls of the Roman town of Pompeii

Wine and food were stored in large vase-shaped jars called amphoras

LIVING IN STYLE

While the poor lived packed together in large apartment blocks known as *insulae*, a wealthy Roman could afford to live in a spacious town house, or *domus*. These homes were peaceful since none of the walls facing the street had windows. The houses were richly decorated with marble panels, columns and statues, expensive paintings on the walls, and mosaics on the floors.

The four roofs sloped inward so the rain filled an ornamental pool inside the house

All the private rooms opened off a central courtyard garden planted with shrubs and flowers

Except for a few couches, chairs, and tables, there was little furniture

MUSIC LOVERS

This mosaic shows an actor beating a tambourine. In Roman times, music was everywhere. It was played in markets and theaters, and at banquets, religious festivals, weddings, and funerals. There were even music competitions in the middle of gladiator shows and chariot races.

Statues of the gods were covered in gold, to show how important they were

Generals built arches to celebrate their victories

Inside the temple was a shrine with a statue of a god or goddess

Priests called augurs looked for good or bad omens by watching the flights of birds

Animals were sacrificed on an altar outside the temple— their organs were burned so the smoke would carry the offering up to the gods

MAKING A SPLASH

In the afternoon, many Romans enjoyed a trip to the baths. This was a great place to freshen up, do business, or just hang out with friends. Slaves were on hand for a relaxing massage, leg wax, or haircut!

The baths were a series of heated rooms that got hotter and hotter

ON A WING AND A PRAYER

Every day, Roman families prayed to their household gods. They were also expected to honor the gods that protected their town. The Romans believed that if the gods got angry, terrible things would happen. So they built splendid temples as homes for them. There, prominent citizens offered animal sacrifices, so the gods would offer help in return.

Gladiator shows were held in round stadiums called amphitheaters

FASHION

The Romans liked to look good. Wealthy women adorned themselves with makeup and jewelry, such as this brooch in the shape of a frog. Many wore wigs, while others had slaves to help them style their hair. Women wore tunics with a long dress on top, and silk outfits and exotic pets were a sign of wealth. Most men wore a simple woolen tunic, but only Roman citizens had the right to wear a toga (a heavy woolen garment that was folded over the shoulder).

FUN AND GAMES

The Romans knew how to relax. They enjoyed music, games such as dice, and trips to the theater. On public holidays, local politicians tried to win votes by providing free gladiator shows. These were brutal, bloody contests in which slaves fought to the death armed with spears and swords. The best gladiators were superstars and had many female fans. They had nicknames such as Tigris ("Tiger") or Montanus ("Highlander").

TEMPLE OF DEATH

It's 700 CE, and the quiet of the Central American rain forest is shattered by shouts, cheers, and the sounds of drums, shell horns, and rattles. The dancing crowd in this Maya city are celebrating a victory over a neighboring tribe. It's a time for prayers, feasting, and bloody rituals. A great cry rings out: "Hail Itzamná, the mighty sky god!" Atop a lofty pyramid, the high priest sacrifices one of the many prisoners of war. Others are paraded below, their fates already sealed.

Teams of men struggle as they hoist a giant new monument in celebration of their victory. Everyone is here to enjoy the party. Nearby a noble lady is carried on a chair of polished wood with pillows of stuffed jaguar skin, her face hidden behind a veil of cotton. The peasants gather below the temple after working long hours in the fields, watching as holy men offer prayers to protect the king.

Merchants from far and wide carry on business as usual in the teeming bazaar on the palace steps. Deals are made using sticks and pebbles in the dirt, and precious items such as polished stone beads, oyster shells, and cocoa beans change hands. There is much to catch the eye— cotton fabrics woven on looms and dyed in bright colors, beautiful pieces of carved jade, pottery figures, and even shells and coral from distant seas. Still weary from battle, warriors smeared in war paint and wearing feathered helmets clutch the clubs and spears that gave them victory. Important nobles bring offerings to the gods, their strings of beads and jade earrings showing their wealth. There's a feast of young sea turtles and pit-roasted deer to come, washed down with honey mead, and fires will soon be lit so the celebrations can last through the night.

THE MIGHTY MAYA

The Maya were avid stargazers who built magnificent temples and palaces that reached up to the stars. But their writings reveal another side: a dark obsession with bloody rituals. In fact, Maya beliefs shaped their cities. The king's palace was built in the heart of the city. Since north was linked to the heavens, where the king's ancestors lived, tombs, pyramids, and temples were built there.

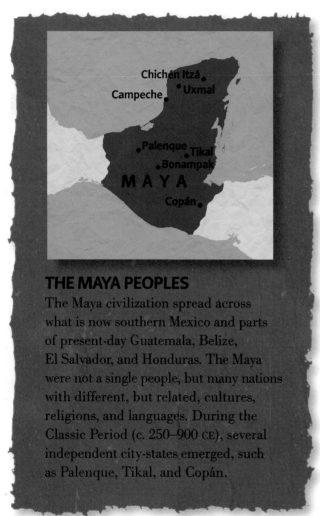

THE MAYA PEOPLES

The Maya civilization spread across what is now southern Mexico and parts of present-day Guatemala, Belize, El Salvador, and Honduras. The Maya were not a single people, but many nations with different, but related, cultures, religions, and languages. During the Classic Period (c. 250–900 CE), several independent city-states emerged, such as Palenque, Tikal, and Copán.

A GIFT OF BLOOD

To the Maya, prayers and rituals were an important part of daily life. Captives and orphans were regularly sacrificed to the gods since the Maya believed this was the only way to keep their gods happy and prevent chaos. Maya nobles also offered their own blood—by jabbing spines through their ears or drawing a string of thorns through their tongues!

The Maya painted their victims blue, then beheaded them or cut their throats—the bodies were hurled down the temple steps

SLASH AND BURN

To grow crops such as corn, sweet potatoes, and cotton, Maya farmers cut down the surrounding jungle, then burned it. The land was only fertile for a few years, then a new area had to be cleared. Raised fields were also built in swamps, watered by canals.

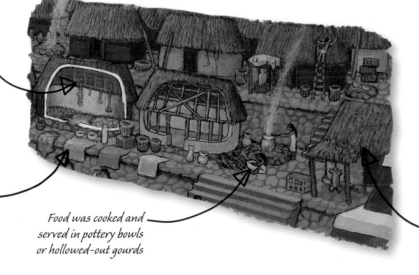

Homes were built with wooden poles and walls of mud or stone

Furniture was simple, such as reed mats, wooden tables, and benches and stools

Food was cooked and served in pottery bowls or hollowed-out gourds

THE OUTDOOR LIFE

Maya peasants lived in simple huts with thatched roofs, built on mounds to keep rainwater from pouring in. These were mainly used for sleeping and storage, since people lived, cooked, and worked outdoors. Nobles had much larger houses and kitchens in separate buildings. While the rich wore fine cotton clothes, peasants dressed in garments made from the softened bark of trees.

The sloping thatch roof soaked up the rain, cooling the house in hot weather

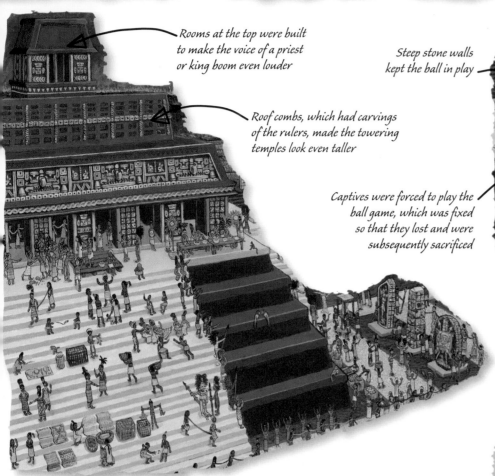

Rooms at the top were built to make the voice of a priest or king boom even louder

Roof combs, which had carvings of the rulers, made the towering temples look even taller

Captives were forced to play the ball game, which was fixed so that they lost and were subsequently sacrificed

Players tried to get the ball through a hoop 26 ft (8 m) off the ground

Steep stone walls kept the ball in play

HEADS YOU LOSE!

Other Maya religious rituals included dancing, music, and sacred ball games. The competing teams symbolized the battles between the gods and the underworld. In some games, the leader of the losing team had his head cut off. His skull would then be used as the core for a new rubber ball! The rubber balls were heavy enough to break bones or even kill the players.

PALACES AND PYRAMIDS

The Maya were impressive engineers. They built buildings from limestone and concrete, including immense palaces and stepped pyramids more than 200 ft (60 m) tall. These were arranged around large plazas filled with a forest of *te-tuns*, or tree stones. These carved monuments honored kings and important events. Buildings were also decorated with intricate carvings on the outside and colorful wall paintings on the inside, which showed scenes of nobles, battles, and sacrifices.

CARVED IN STONE

The Maya were one of the few Native American peoples to develop a full writing system. It was very complex, with hundreds of unique symbols, known as glyphs. The symbols were carved into stone or written in books made from bark paper. Probably only nobles and priests were able to read them.

TIMEKEEPERS

Maya priests looked to the heavens for guidance. They were skilled astronomers who used simple devices to track the movement of the sun, stars, and planets. They built observatories (right) to watch the sun rise and set, and to mark the longest and shortest days of the year. Their calculations allowed them to create a calendar of 365 days per year. A year was divided into 18 months of 20 days—plus 5 unlucky days with no name.

A HOME FOR THE DEAD

The Maya placed two objects in the mouths of their dead: a piece of corn to serve as food for the long journey to the heavens and a stone bead to pay the toll to get there. Bodies were wrapped in cotton and painted red, the color of death. While peasants were buried in simple graves under the floors of houses, priests and nobles were buried inside pyramids, along with their favorite possessions.

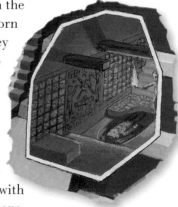

VIKING PORT

It's all hustle and bustle down by the waterfront in Hedeby. Women pound their laundry at the water's edge, goods are lifted from the ships docked along the quay, and merchants argue loudly over a group of blond slaves. But the Arab traveler is not impressed. It is 900 CE and although Hedeby is one of the largest towns in the region, it is rough, dirty, and dangerous. Wisely, he keeps his thoughts to himself. The farmers here are also vicious pirates feared across Europe, where they are known by another name—Vikings!

Ugh! The first thing that strikes the visitor is the smell. Hedeby lies at the southern end of the Ox Road used by the Vikings, or Norsemen, to drive their cattle south to Germany, and animal dung litters the streets. It's also a fishing town, and the stink of rotting fish guts hangs in the air, mingling with the foul stench of shoemaker's leather soaked in urine. And what a noise! Shipbuilders and blacksmiths hammer loudly in the background, while a pig runs squealing through the quayside. All of a sudden, a fierce roar goes up as a raiding party sets off in search of loot, as if the dragon's head on their ship isn't scary enough! The locals hardly notice. Amid the din, two neighbors calmly play backgammon in the spring sunshine. Pausing to scold a slave, a high-ranking official parades through town dripping in gold, his flashing eyes circled by a ring of coal-black makeup. Foreign merchants in colorful clothes seek out furs from Russia, soapstone bowls from the Scottish isles, German glass for bracelets, Spanish wine, and silver and silks from the east. Despite their fearsome reputation, there's a lot more to Vikings than booty, burning, and bloodshed!

A PLACE TO TRADE

Although the Vikings were great storytellers, they didn't write things down in books. Luckily, they did like to bury silver and everyday items, so many Viking objects have survived. We also know about the Vikings from travelers, such as the Arab merchant Al-Tartushi who visited Hedeby (and hated it) in 950 CE. You can still walk along the rampart that defended the town, and archeologists have dug up the remains of Viking houses preserved in its soggy soil.

VIKING SETTLEMENTS

The Vikings came from Scandinavia, the lands that are now Sweden, Denmark, and Norway. During the 8th century CE, the Vikings carried out daring raids across northern Europe. Starting in the 9th century, they settled in England, Ireland, Iceland, Greenland, and Russia. They also sailed south to plunder or trade with Spain, Italy, and Constantinople, and west to America.

BRING YOUR BOOTS

Hedeby was probably pretty run-down, with muddy, waterlogged streets surfaced with split logs and few large public buildings. Viking houses were made from wattle and daub and had thatched roofs. Most didn't last more than 30 years. When a house fell down, another was built on top. Inside, the houses were very simple with a fire for cooking, and raised benches covered with fur or cloth. These were used as work spaces by day and beds at night.

SEA LORDS

The Vikings were master shipbuilders. Pride of the fleet were the dragon-headed longships used for raids deep into enemy territory. Like all Viking ships, they were pointed at the ends and wide in the middle. They could be rowed up shallow rivers or even hauled across land. A more common sight in Hedeby were the bulky knarrs used for long-distance trade, which relied on their sails, and smaller boats used for fishing.

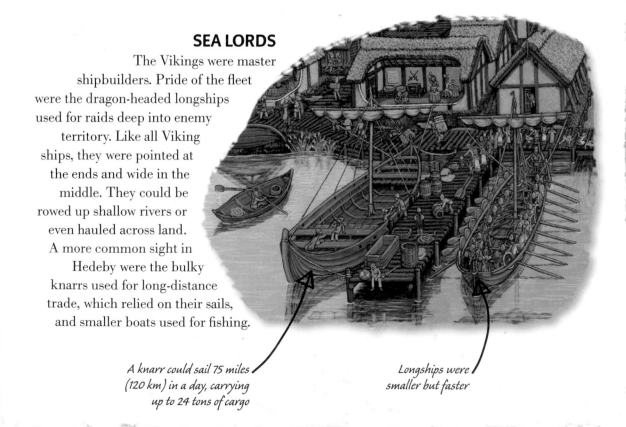

A knarr could sail 75 miles (120 km) in a day, carrying up to 24 tons of cargo

Longships were smaller but faster

MYSTERIOUS RUNES

The Vikings didn't have books, but they did have an alphabet of 16 letters, or runes. These were carved in wood, bone, or stone, then colored in with black, red, or white paint. The runes were used on gravestones, and to make lists, write poetry, and even cast spells!

BOAT BURIALS

When they died, the Vikings were buried or burned in small boats for the journey to the afterlife, along with food, clothes, and their personal belongings. Wealthy people were buried with a whole longship. At Hedeby, rich and poor were buried alongside each other, and in time, houses and shops were often built on top of the graves.

Metalwork was seen as a "magical" skill in Viking times, partly because blacksmiths carefully guarded the secrets of their craft

This ship is being hauled to the burial ground, where after the burial it will be covered in a mound of earth

MOBILE ART

Vikings were violent and sometimes bloodthirsty, but they were also very artistic. Often on the move, they carried their art with them, such as decorated drinking horns and carved paddles. Norse metalworkers created fine weapons and glittering jewelry, while sculptors carved fantastic animal shapes and intricate patterns on amber, bone, walrus ivory, and wood.

KILLED FOR THE GODS

The Vikings were very superstitious and prayed to gods such as Odin and Thor, who lived in the heavenly city of Asgard. If treated well, the gods would help protect them from evil forces and bring a good harvest. The Vikings usually worshipped their gods in the open air, by sacrificing animals (and even humans) to them.

Dead horses, cattle, rams, billy goats, or pigs were hung on poles as an offering to the gods

Arab traders came in search of amber jewelry, fox-fur caps and coats, and blond slaves

Viking jarls showed off their wealth by wearing jewelry such as twisted neck rings, or wearing highly decorated swords

Thralls did the dirty jobs around town and could even be "put down" by their owners if they were sick or injured

Fishermen, shipwrights, metalworkers, carpenters, craftsmen, and farmers were usually freemen

VIKING SILVER

The Vikings loved silver, a symbol of wealth and power. Although they minted their own coins, they didn't use them to trade. Viking merchants carried small folding scales that were very accurate, so large pieces of jewelry were often chopped up into smaller pieces to make up the exact weight of silver required to finish a deal.

A MAN'S WORLD?

Viking society was divided into jarls (chiefs and military leaders), karls (freemen), and thralls (slaves). The slaves were usually captured during raids and sold and bought by the Vikings like cattle. The owner could treat a slave however he wanted. The more land, money, and slaves a Viking had, the more important his family was. Women were not as free as men. However, they ran the farm while their husbands were away, and although girls could not choose a husband, if he treated her badly, she could divorce him.

SPRING FESTIVAL

Business in China is booming under the Song emperors. Advances in farming and industry mean that rich and poor alike can enjoy public festivals such as this Qingming Festival, when families honor their dead relatives by sweeping their graves. Tempting smells from stalls, teahouses, and restaurants draw the crowds into town. The air is filled with the cracks and pops of fireworks and the crashing cymbals and gongs of the spectacular dragon dance. It's time to celebrate!

Europe in the 11th century is a rough-and-tumble world of knights, castles, and crusades. But in Song Dynasty China the clash of swords has been replaced by the hubbub of the marketplace. Traveling salesmen balancing baskets on their shoulders skip nimbly around camels and donkeys laden with goods, while the broad streets, busy restaurants, and tall buildings are all signs that times are good.

The river acts as a highway, linking the town to the rest of the sprawling Chinese empire. Its flowing waters power water mills and flood the rice fields. Close to the river bank, a fisherman casts his net. More food means more people and, by the 12th century, Chinese cities are bursting at the seams. The store-lined streets are thronged with people. Many wear simple jackets and coats made of coarse cotton, while

the wealthy sweep by in elegant silk robes and dresses. Stalls and teahouses are doing brisk business. In the surrounding workshops, craftsmen are hard at work producing silk, paper, and porcelain goods. It's "all systems go" as merchants get down to business amid a sea of porters, storytellers, fortune-tellers, doctors, scholars, and monks.

MEDIEVAL CHINA

The Qingming scroll, painted around 1100, gives us an amazing snapshot of Chinese daily life at this time. Around 170 years later, Italian explorer Marco Polo wrote in wonder about China's technological achievements: Paper money, gunpowder, printing, and the magnetic compass were all invented under the Song emperors.

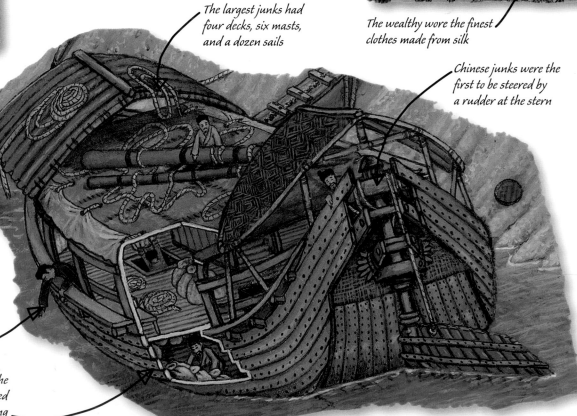

Dragons are symbols of power and courage, and are seen as sacred animals in China

The dance drives away evil spirits, bringing good fortune to the local people

LUCKY DRAGON

Dragon dances have been performed at festivals and other big occasions since the time of the Han emperors (206 BCE–220 CE). Nine or more dancers coordinate their movements so that the tail and head of the dragon move together.

SONG DYNASTY

During the Song Dynasty (960–1279), the population in China doubled to 100 million people (half the people in the world). Many lived along the Yangzte River. The two largest cities, Haifeng and Hangzhou, were both home to more than a million people.

Haifeng

ON THE MOVE

Rich women often rode in covered sedan chairs carried by servants. They had little choice, due to the custom of foot binding, which made it painful to walk. While officials and scholars traveled on horseback, most people got around on foot. Donkeys and oxen were used to take heavy goods to market.

The wealthy wore the finest clothes made from silk

The largest junks had four decks, six masts, and a dozen sails

Chinese junks were the first to be steered by a rudder at the stern

HIGH-TECH JUNK

Chinese ships, known as junks, were marvels of medieval engineering. The largest vessels, up to 82 ft (25 m) long, could carry more than 100 tons of rice. A system of canals allowed junks to sail far inland. Some medieval Chinese junks were huge—more than five times the size of European vessels.

Chinese sailors were the first to navigate using charts and magnetic compasses, and by collecting samples of mud from the seabed

Watertight compartments in the hull could keep a damaged junk from sinking

ENJOYING THE FESTIVAL

During the Qingming Festival, families swept the graves of dead relatives. It was also a time of celebration: People went to teahouses, restaurants, or all-day social clubs, where they could enjoy poetry, music, and games such as Go. This was a board game played by two people that involved a lot of strategic thinking.

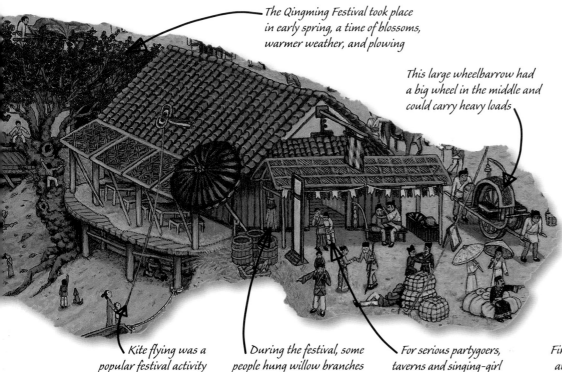

The Qingming Festival took place in early spring, a time of blossoms, warmer weather, and plowing

This large wheelbarrow had a big wheel in the middle and could carry heavy loads

Kite flying was a popular festival activity

During the festival, some people hung willow branches to ward off evil spirits

For serious partygoers, taverns and singing-girl houses were open until the early hours of the morning

PRINTING

Paper was first invented in China in 105 CE by mixing finely chopped mulberry bark and hemp rags with water, mashing it flat, then leaving the mix to dry out in the sun. Although the Qingming scroll (above) and other works of art were drawn or painted by hand, books were also printed at this time using either movable type or by carving whole pages onto wooden plates.

Firecrackers were also used to drive away evil spirits—the gunpowder that made them explode was first invented in China

Buildings were made of wood with a tiled roof

PAPER MONEY

In the 11th century, the Song government was minting six billion coins a year and running out of copper. They came up with a clever solution—the world's first official paper banknotes. These were printed with intricate designs. Anyone caught forging notes had their head cut off!

OPEN 24 HOURS

From dawn until late in the evening, stalls and shops sold anything and everything: wine, grain, gold and silver, shoes, weapons, lanterns, toys, porcelain, fabric, and medicine. Delicious snacks were also available around the clock, from the bars selling breakfast delicacies such as dumplings and soups to noodle shops that were open all night. Cakes, fruit juices (lychee and pear), and honey and ginger drinks were also popular, and during the Qingming Festival people ate date dumplings.

MEDIEVAL VILLAGE

Harvest time in 15th-century France is one of the busiest times of the year. Men, women, and children work together to cut the wheat with sickles, then bundle it into sheaves, ready to be pitchforked into a cart and hauled off to the barns. Later, the grain is taken to the water mill to be ground into flour. In the coming weeks there are apples to be picked and grapes to be trodden to make wine. For a medieval peasant, it's work, work, work.

During the medieval period (from about 1000 to 1500), beautiful castles, cathedrals, and abbeys are built. Bloody wars are fought between knights, and trade flourishes in the towns. But while the rich, like the lord and his lady crossing the bridge, live in great castles of stone, most people, the peasants, live in villages. There's no school, and children help their parents in the fields, picking apples, scaring birds away, or driving ducks to the pond. Most of the work takes place in the large open fields where every farmer in the village has his own strips of land. To keep the soil fertile, a field is sown with wheat one year, beans the next, then left unplanted, or fallow, during the third year. Most crops are used to feed the family or pay rent to the local lord. In a good year, the surplus can be sold, and money can also be made by carting wood for fuel.

Any money left over can be spent at stalls in the village run by traveling merchants or peddlers, or at the local tavern. At the edge of the village is common land where anyone can graze their cattle. These provide the family with milk, butter, and cheese, while a few sheep provide wool for clothing. In fact, life in the country is far healthier than in the towns, where disease spreads like wildfire.

PEASANT LIFE

Life for peasants was tough. Starting in childhood, they worked long hours in the fields, rain or shine. They ate well when harvests were good, but starved if they failed. Death was always close by: Deadly diseases struck every few years, women often died giving birth, and one in four children died in their first year. But it wasn't all doom and gloom. Work stopped on holy days, Christmas, and Easter, a time for feasting, plays, soccer, dancing, cockfighting, music, and drinking.

KINGS, LORDS, AND VILLEINS

During the medieval period, society in Europe was feudal. Kings owned all the land, which was granted to lords in return for service in war. They in turn rented the land to knights for their support and so on down to the peasants, or villeins, who were granted a few acres of land in return for work or payments of money, animals, or goods. As a result, most peasants worked on land they did not own.

Medieval lords built heavily fortified stone castles to control the surrounding countryside

Peasant farmers worked alongside each other on strips of land scattered across two or three large fields

MEDIEVAL FRANCE

France in the 15th century was a patchwork of regions controlled by powerful lords such as the Dukes of Burgundy, Brittany, and Berry. Some were loyal to the king; others were not. Wealthy church leaders such as abbots and bishops also controlled large estates. By 1475, however, the French king had a strong grip over most of France.

CREATURE COMFORTS

At home, a peasant woman did everything, from making clothes and collecting firewood to cooking, doing laundry, and looking after the children. But one or two peasant families in every village were rich enough to dress in fine clothes and own luxury items such as combs (above) and mirrors.

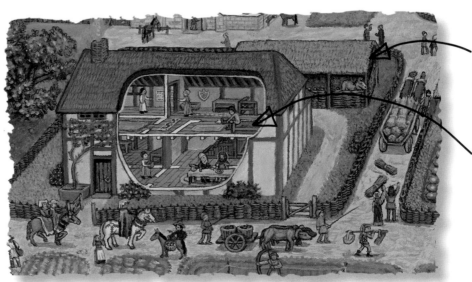

Grooms slept in the stables with the horses

While lords and ladies slept in private rooms upstairs, most travelers slept on wooden pallets on the floor

BEWARE THE BANDITS!

The right to farm a strip of land was inherited by the eldest son, so younger brothers often left home to make a living. Although peasants didn't visit each other much, they traveled to markets on foot or by donkey and made pilgrimages to holy shrines. Bandits were a constant threat so pilgrims from all walks of life traveled in groups. On the way, they stayed at inns, with millers, merchants, and knights all under the same roof.

MEDIEVAL MACHINES

From the 12th century onward, a wave of new technology appeared in Europe, from cranes, wheelbarrows, and windmills to eyeglasses, mechanical clocks, and gunpowder. Most medieval villages had water mills to grind grain or used the power of flowing water to saw timber, raise stones from mine shafts, sharpen tools, or crush stone and metal.

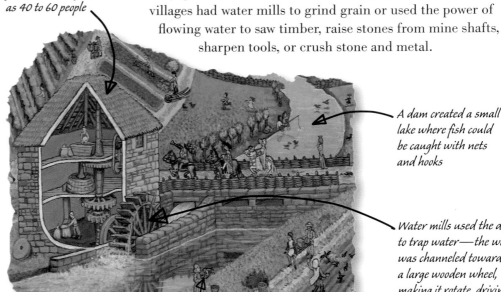

A water mill could grind as much grain as 40 to 60 people

A dam created a small lake where fish could be caught with nets and hooks

Water mills used the dam to trap water—the water was channeled toward a large wooden wheel, making it rotate, driving the machinery inside the mill

Falconry, using tamed birds of prey to hunt waterfowl and small game, was popular in medieval Europe

THE SEASONS

Village life revolved around the seasons, as illustrated in the *Très Riches Heures* (*Three Rich Hours*), painted for the Duke of Berry between 1410 and 1489. Midwinter was a time of rest (above), but once spring arrived the hard work began— sowing, plowing, and harrowing the fields. The harvest was in summer, while most animals were slaughtered in late autumn.

Peasant homes weren't tiny hovels, but they were often smoky, cold, and damp

Churches were also used as courtrooms or as a place to store grain, keep sheep, or brew wine

THE BOOK REVOLUTION

In 1455, Johann Gutenberg's Bible became the first major book printed with a printing press and movable type. Before this, books were copied by hand onto vellum (calf- or lambskin) rather than paper. Gutenberg's invention made printing faster and cheaper, and printing presses soon sprang up all over Europe. By 1501, 20 million books had been printed. Most people did not know how to read, however, so traveling storytellers made a living by reading books out loud.

THE PARISH CHURCH

The church was the center of village life—baptisms, weddings, and funerals were all celebrated here. On Sunday, everyone went to church wearing their best clothes. The church bells also summoned villagers to hear important news or to warn of danger. Although the priest played a very important role, he was expected to work the church lands. He was also supported by local peasants who paid a tenth of everything they earned, known as tithes.

CITY OF GOLD

It's 1500, and Timbuktu is known as the Pearl of Africa with good reason. After 60 years of turmoil, peace and prosperity have returned to the city. Yes, the narrow streets may be ankle-deep in sand, and the mud-brick houses that line them may look ordinary, but don't be fooled. The fine clothes and glittering jewelry worn by many locals give away the secret: There's money here—lots of it! Timbuktu is at the crossroads of the desert and the Niger River, and wealthy merchants travel great distances to trade gold and salt.

From the minaret of the Great Mosque, a call to prayer echoes across the rooftops. For Timbuktu is also a holy city and a place of learning. Its streets are filled with doctors, lawyers, and countless other scholars. Voices are raised in heated debate, but no one dares to make trouble. The emperor has an army of thousands, including mounted knights, and archers who shoot poison arrows.

City life revolves around the two central markets. They are a feast for the senses. A stubborn camel groans loudly as blocks of salt the size of tombstones are unloaded from its back. Heavenly scents waft through the air, thanks to the spices, perfumes, fine cloths, and silks spread out on the ground. Books are bought and sold for huge sums. Near the Great Mosque, goats, cattle, sheep,

and ostriches can all fetch a good price, along with fresh fish caught with nets in the Niger. The eye is dazzled by a parade of colorful caftans, turbans, and head scarves, as Arab traders rub shoulders with desert nomads—Tuaregs and Berbers—and the Malinke people of west Africa. No wonder Timbuktu's fame has even reached London and Paris!

A PORT IN THE DESERT

In the 1100s, Timbuktu was a travelers' camp used by desert nomads. By the 1300s, it had grown into a thriving metropolis as well as a center for Islamic scholarship and culture. It was like a port in the desert—gold, slaves, and ivory were brought by canoe from west Africa along the Niger River. Arab merchants traded salt, horses, and silk for these goods, then shipped them north across the desert using teams of camels, known as caravans.

Slaves were yoked together by the neck

Traders sat under homemade sunshades with their goods spread out on the ground

Armed guards kept order in the marketplace

Each slab of rock salt weighed more than 55 lb (25 kg)

SALT FOR GOLD
Starting in the 1300s, caravans with thousands of camels headed across the desert sands to Timbuktu, carrying glass, perfume, daggers, beads, fine Egyptian fabrics, and huge slabs of salt. Without this precious cargo, cut from the rock at Taoudenni in the Sahara, the desert peoples couldn't survive. Salt was exchanged for gold from west Africa, mined from pits up to 49 ft (15 m) deep, as well as leather, cotton, kola nuts, and millet (a grain). Slaves were also traded—but many would die on the punishing walk across the Sahara Desert.

SAHARAN MARKET TOWN
Timbuktu clings to the edge of the Sahara Desert, about eight miles (13 km) north of a bend in the Niger River. Now in the African country of Mali, during the 15th and 16th centuries it was part of the Songhai Empire. The surrounding countryside was bare, but Timbuktu's unique location, at the crossroads of the salt and gold trade, lured merchants from Tunis to Djenné.

The main courtyard had a number of stalls for storing goods and resting camels— the merchants slept upstairs

The high walls of the funduq kept the traders and their goods safe from robbers at night

The entrance was tall, to allow heavily laden camels, the ships of the desert, to enter

KING MUSA
In 1324, Mansa Musa, the king of Mali, set off on a 6,000-mile (9,500 km) pilgrimage to Mecca. Stopping in Cairo, he gave away so much gold that the Egyptian money market was ruined for 10 years! His fame spread to Europe, and in 1375 Abraham Creques, a Spanish mapmaker, showed Musa on his map, holding a gold nugget.

ROOM AT THE INN
Some of the busiest places in Timbuktu would have been the travelers' inns, or funduqs, where merchants could rest and recover after a long journey. A funduq supplied food for people and fodder for animals, as well as water for both drinking and washing—Muslims performed a sacred wash five times a day before praying. Travelers could also buy supplies here for the trip home.

The call to prayer was made from the top of a minaret (tower), which had a staircase inside

There was enough prayer space inside the Great Mosque for 2,000 people

THE GREAT MOSQUE

Muhammed, the founder of Islam, was born around 570 CE in Arabia. By the 800s, most of the Arab merchants crossing the Sahara were Muslims (followers of Islam) and brought their religion to Timbuktu. Returning from his great pilgrimage to Mecca, the Malian king Mansa Musa brought many scholars back to Timbuktu with him, including the gifted architect Abu Ishaq Al-Saheli. Musa gave Al-Saheli a huge sum of gold to design and build the Jingaray Ber, the Great Mosque, and a splendid palace for himself.

MEDIEVAL MANUSCRIPTS

A staggering 700,000 sacred manuscripts, some dating back 600 years, still survive in Timbuktu, many buried for centuries under the desert sand. The books are covered in sheep- or goatskin and many contain hundreds of pages of beautiful Arabic handwriting. They reveal the wide range of subjects studied in medieval Timbuktu, from astronomy and math to history, medicine, and law.

Cooking was usually done in a small courtyard or out in the street

Fresh bread was baked in beehive-shaped clay ovens

DARK AND STUFFY

Most houses in Timbuktu were simple dwellings made from brick. Their flat roofs had drains built from split palm trunks for the rainy season. The rooms inside were narrow and dark. There was also very little furniture. Rich merchants lived in houses made of stone, often with elaborate wooden doors with large rings for knockers. Poor people lived in domed huts made of branches with a covering of matting, many on the outskirts of the city.

A wicker bed and thin mattress of rushes or reeds were often the only furniture

Students were often taught out in the open

A CITY OF LEARNING

By the 1450s, there were around 25,000 students in Timbuktu, many of whom had studied in Egypt or Mecca. The city had more than 180 schools and three universities, organized around the three great mosques of Jingaray Ber, Sidi Yahya, and Sankore. Students studied the Quran in Arabic under teachers known as marabouts, and were expected to memorize large portions of the holy book.

SANKORE MOSQUE

While the Great Mosque has been rebuilt many times, the original Sankore Mosque still stands. Built around a wooden frame, its posts are like a scaffolding, making it easier to repair the damage caused by the annual rains. The mosque was the center of a university. Some scholars taught in the open courtyards of the mosque, while others passed on their knowledge of trades such as carpentry and fishing.

SULTAN'S PALACE

In 17th-century Istanbul, an anxious courtier adjusts his turban as he hurries across the palace courtyard. The other courtiers are already waiting for the sultan in neat lines. Beside them stand rows of fearsome Janissaries, the sultan's bodyguards, while mounted archers show off their skills. A loud blast from the marching band announces that the sultan is on his way, interrupting the prayers of the faithful in the mosque, and distracting the young boys in the far courtyard from their studies. There's not a moment to lose. The courtier prays he will catch the sultan's eye, for nothing can be done without his permission.

No city in the Ottoman Empire is more splendid than Istanbul. The heart of the city is the sprawling Topkapi Palace, which sits high above the Bosphorus, the gateway between the Black Sea and the Aegean. Home to the sultan and 4,000 others, the palace is a city within a city, with its own mosques, schools, libraries, workshops, hospitals, military barracks, kitchens, and gardens. It is built around four great courtyards. Anyone can enter the first since the law courts are here, but the second courtyard is open only to those on official business. Here are government buildings such as the treasury and the Divan (the imperial council room). The sultan's headquarters are in the third and fourth courtyards. Although the courtiers wait patiently in line, when their lord passes through the Gate of Felicity, they will cry out and wave their folded petitions over their heads. The lucky ones will have their wishes granted. For within the palace walls, the sultan is a godlike master, to whom no one speaks without first being spoken to. Many of the palace inhabitants are slaves, including the women of the harem and the many soldiers who guard its high walls. Even the sultan's own brothers, all rivals to the throne, are kept under lock and key.

A CITY WITHIN A CITY

The Topkapi Palace contained all that was needed to give the sultan a life of luxury, from hunting grounds to baths and fountains. But the palace was also a place of work. Astronomers gazed at the stars, hammers fell and sparks flew in the many workshops, while a thousand cooks toiled in the kitchens.

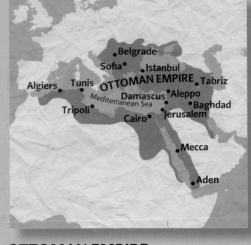

OTTOMAN EMPIRE

At the height of its power in the mid-16th century, the Ottomans controlled large areas of southeastern Europe, western Asia, and north Africa. The capital, Istanbul, formerly the Byzantine city of Constantinople, had been captured in 1453. During the 16th and 17th centuries, the empire prospered under a line of dynamic sultans. Thanks to a powerful navy, the Ottomans also controlled much of the Mediterranean Sea.

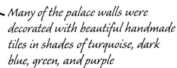

Behind this wall, a secret passage ran from the gate to the sultan's Divan

When ambassadors came to see the sultan in the Chamber of Petitions, they were expected to kiss the hem of his skirt

The gate's double doors enclosed a small space in which condemned prisoners were strangled to death

On important occasions, the sultan sat in front of the gate on his gold-plated throne

Many of the palace walls were decorated with beautiful handmade tiles in shades of turquoise, dark blue, green, and purple

THE GATE OF DEATH

The third courtyard was entered through the Gate of Felicity. Except for the individuals who were invited for an audience with the sultan in the Chamber of Petitions, no one passed this point without his permission. If they pleased the sultan, he showered them with gifts and titles. If not, he might have them strangled to death! Beyond the Chamber of Petitions was the Inner Palace, where the sultan spent most of his days and silence had to be observed at all times.

Courtiers gathered in the second courtyard to await the arrival of the sultan

A LIFE OF DUTY

The Topkapi Palace was also the center of government. The clerks of the treasury organized the empire's finances, and nearby was the Imperial Divan, where senior officials (the Imperial Council) held meetings. Some of these officials had spent all of their lives in the palace, starting as page boys for the sultan. They were taught subjects such as music, painting, and handwriting in a school in the third courtyard.

THE MIGHTY GARDENER

The officials of the court ran the army and the empire. They had titles such as Chief Standard Bearer, Great Master of the Horse, and Head Falconer. Most powerful of all was the Chief Gardener, with 2,000 men under his control, including the palace watchmen, grooms, and the sultan's bodyguards and entertainers. Even he had to wait in line to see the sultan and needed his permission to pass through the Gate of Felicity.

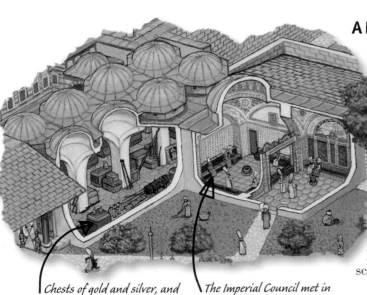

Chests of gold and silver, and weapons covered in jewels were stored in the treasury

The Imperial Council met in the Divan four times a week, after prayer at dawn

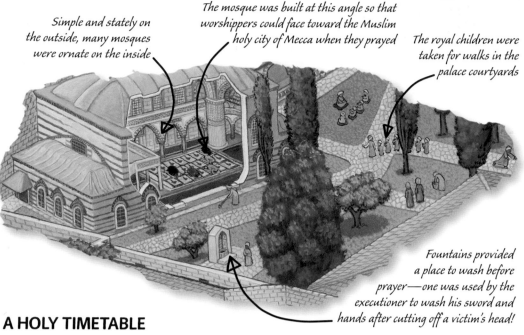

Simple and stately on the outside, many mosques were ornate on the inside

The mosque was built at this angle so that worshippers could face toward the Muslim holy city of Mecca when they prayed

The royal children were taken for walks in the palace courtyards

Fountains provided a place to wash before prayer—one was used by the executioner to wash his sword and hands after cutting off a victim's head!

A HOLY TIMETABLE

Like all Muslims, the Ottomans prayed five times a day and the palace had several mosques. Daily life was regulated by the hours of prayer so there was no need for clocks, although there were sundials on public walls and water clocks in some mosques. Washing was a very important part of the daily ritual and a vast system of aqueducts, water towers, and underground cisterns fed the palace's drinking fountains, baths, and gardens.

WHO GOES THERE?

Thousands of soldiers lived in the palace including the sultan's personal bodyguards, the Janissaries. Janissaries were slaves from eastern Europe. The Ottomans took them as children from Christian families as part of a tax, then brought them up as Muslims.

Mounted soldiers practiced archery in the palace grounds

POETRY AND ART

The Ottomans had a great love of art and beauty. Miniature paintings and illuminated manuscripts were often crafted for the sultan, like this book of poetry. The designer-painters were expected to record important events such as victories, festivals, and processions. Ottoman calligraphers wrote the swirling Arabic script in books and on the distinctive blue tiles that adorned the walls of mosques, palaces, and tombs.

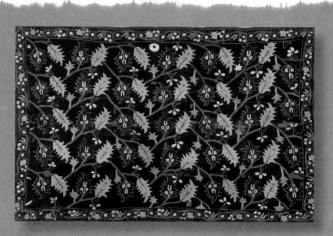

HANGING CARPET

Ottoman rooms, even those in the sultan's palace, had very little furniture apart from little square mattresses or heaps of velvet or wool cushions dotted around the room, and long padded seats called divans along the walls. Carpets were found in all homes. Some were for sleeping on, others for prayer, while the most beautiful (like the one above) were hung on the walls for display and insulation. During the hot summer months, carpets on the floor were replaced by rush mats.

The women of the harem were guarded by slaves from Africa and eastern Europe

When young girls arrived in the harem, they were taught poetry, dancing, and the many rules of the palace

DO NOT ENTER

The most private area in the palace was the harem, a maze of often-small rooms. Except for the sultan and those who guarded the women, the only men allowed in were visiting relatives. Most of the women in the harem were foreign slaves bought at the age of 10 or 11. If the sultan took a fancy to a woman, she was given her own apartment. If she bore him a child, she became his wife. As a result, the harem was a hotbed of plotting as mothers tried to ensure that their daughters became the sultan's wife.

TALE OF TWO CITIES

Here in the 1730s, an Austrian town is celebrating Christmas. In cities such as Vienna and Salzburg, grand Baroque houses sit beside towering Gothic cathedrals. There is the clatter of hooves on the cobbled streets as wagons and carriages rumble by. Ladies in their finery browse in stores selling wigs, hats, and porcelain. Gentlemen gather in coffeehouses to read the newspaper or strike a deal. The gentle tinkling of a harpsichord drifts down onto the street from a salon window. If you have money, this is a great place to live.

Thanks to spreading empires in the New World and the Far East, many European countries in the 1700s grow wealthy. But not everyone benefits. Poor chimney sweeps and other laborers survive on a meager diet of bread, cabbages, and beans, and eat from wooden or pewter bowls. They live in cramped, dirty, and often damp conditions. In contrast, the wealthy minority live in magnificent houses with glass windows, chandeliers, and elegant furniture, and eat with forks from china plates. Servants attend to their every need, while sedan chairs and horse-drawn carriages whisk them from one place to another. For the rich, life is a never-ending social whirl of card games, balls, salons, and concerts. Such gatherings are opportunities for polite conversation, genteel dances, the latest fashions, and showing off. But the world is changing. Both rich and poor go to church less. Science and technology are everywhere, from the man peering through his telescope to the printing press next to the coffeehouse that churns out a stream of pamphlets and newspapers. More and more people are reading: Books of proverbs are popular. Educated people believe that learning and reason alone can solve the world's problems, so this period is called the Age of Reason, or the Enlightenment.

THE AGE OF ELEGANCE

Although Austria was at war for large parts of the 18th century, cities such as Vienna and Salzburg prospered and were known throughout Europe as centers of music and for their outstanding palaces, churches, and gardens. These were influenced by Baroque ideas, such as grand spectacles and enjoying beauty and pleasure—in other words, showing off and having fun!

18TH CENTURY AUSTRIA

The 18th century was a golden age for Austria despite several long wars. By 1718, the Habsburg king of Austria, Charles VI, ruled over an empire that stretched from northern Italy to Poland and included parts of Hungary and Romania. Meanwhile, the Ottoman Empire, which had besieged Vienna in 1683, was pushed back to Belgrade.

UPSTAIRS, DOWNSTAIRS

Most 18th-century city dwellers lived in small rooms and overcrowded houses with very simple furniture. They went out to have fun: to taverns, theaters, coffeehouses, and pleasure gardens. The wealthy lived in luxurious town houses stuffed with elegant and comfortable furniture, exquisite clocks, and beautiful instruments. In contrast, their servants lived in small, cramped attic rooms.

The sparsely furnished attic rooms were too cold in winter and too hot in summer

In the homes of the wealthy, bedrooms were decorated with luxurious Chinese wallpapers, while the beds and windows were hung with eastern textiles

HAVING A BALL

If you were well-off in the 18th century, there were many ways to spend your spare time: reading, playing cards, going to the theater, or attending a lavish ball. Rich ladies also invited politicians, writers, artists, and scientists to their homes to discuss the latest ideas and enjoy performances by poets, actors, and musicians. These gatherings, known as salons, were one of the few occasions when women were treated as equals by men.

Porcelain was the height of fashion—not just vases and small figures, but mirror frames, clock cases, and even small tables

Fans were not only an essential item for ladies in a crowded, stuffy ballroom; they were also used to send secret messages across the room!

Men wore a frock coat, a waistcoat, and breeches (knee-length leggings)

Learning the minuet or the waltz was a must for the middle classes

Wealthy women competed with each other to invite the most interesting guests

The wealthy enjoyed reading (the first novels were written around this time)

Card games such as whist and quadrille were very popular

FOLLOWERS OF FASHION

For those who could afford it, wearing the latest fashions was a great way to show off. Ladies wore a loose gown over hooped petticoats that grew bigger and bigger. Hair was worn in giant towers known as fontanges. These sometimes caught fire, since most homes were lit by candles. White makeup, worn by both men and women, could poison the wearer because it contained lead and mercury, while tiny pieces of cloth, called patches, were worn on the face to cover up smallpox scars.

Magnificent baroque churches were another way for cities to show off their wealth

The 18th century saw the arrival of banks, such as the Wiener Stadt-Banco (the town bank of Vienna)

The first Christmas markets were held in Austria more than 700 years ago and are still famous today

Soldiers were a familiar sight on city streets, especially near the palace or escorting the royal coach

SIGN OF THE TIMES

Elegant town houses, wide streets, and leafy squares made 18th-century cities beautiful to look at. Many towns were still dominated by a few wealthy families who owned much of the land. They rented houses to bankers, merchants, and lawyers, and shops to artisans and shopkeepers. During the day, the streets were full of life, as soldiers mingled with market traders, and rich men and women paraded in fine clothes. But at night, robbers and gangs ruled the streets of many towns since there were no police forces.

In many cities, printing presses were housed close to coffee shops where their readers congregated

Coffeehouses were like clubs, where businessmen struck deals, exchanged news, and swapped gossip

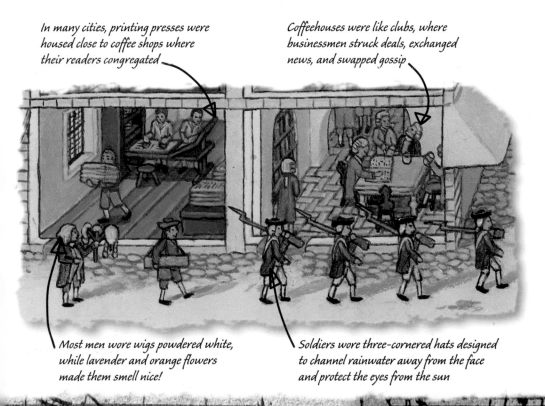

Most men wore wigs powdered white, while lavender and orange flowers made them smell nice!

Soldiers wore three-cornered hats designed to channel rainwater away from the face and protect the eyes from the sun

MUSICAL TRADITION

The arts were supported by both the Roman Catholic Church and the Habsburg emperors—several of them, including Charles VI, were skilled musicians—while the salons welcomed famous composers, such as Wolfgang Amadeus Mozart, who was born in Salzburg in 1756. Many 18th-century instruments survive today, including this violin, which belonged to Mozart.

THE WIENER ZEITUNG

The first newspaper was printed in German-speaking Strasbourg in 1605, and by 1703 Vienna had its own newspaper, the *Wiener Zeitung*, one of the oldest papers in the world and still in print today. It contained regional and international news. However, local news continued to be announced on the street by a town crier or drummer.

EXOTIC TASTES

In the late 17th century, three new drinks changed the drinking habits of Europe: coffee, tea, and chocolate. The first coffeehouse in Austria opened in Vienna in 1683, thanks to a sack of coffee beans left behind by the Ottoman invaders. The Polish officer who opened it, Jerzy Franciszek Kulczycki, popularized the idea of adding milk and sugar. Soon there were dozens of coffeehouses in every European city.

PARTY BY THE SEA

It's late autumn on the west coast of Canada in the early 1800s. The local peoples, the Kwakwaka'wakw, have spent the summer fishing and gathering wild fruits and shellfish. With enough food stored for winter, there's time for a celebration, or potlatch. The chief's daughter is getting married! Messages have been sent out to other villages nearby, and the guests have started to arrive. The party has already started. There's singing, dancing, storytelling—and mountains of food. It's good manners to stuff yourself silly, and by the time the party is over, the ground will be covered in a carpet of clamshells.

Here on the Pacific coast, daily life revolves around the sea, the forests, and the seasons, as it has for thousands of years. Finding food is a big part of everyone's daily routine, whether they're hunting and fishing in canoes or digging blue camas roots out of the ground with a stick. Other activities include blanket and basket weaving, wood carving, and canoe building. As the guests arrive for the potlatch, they will all receive presents from the chief, such as carved wooden boxes, woven baskets, and fur robes. A visiting chief might receive a Chilkat blanket or even a canoe. The more the chief gives away, the more important he is. He leads the potlatch in a carved headdress decorated with fur and sea-lion whiskers, while other dancers wear masks shaped like ravens and wolves. Drums, flutes, and rattles provide the music, and the dancers act out stories. On the beach, a woman is preparing salmon and seaweed stew for the celebration in a cooking box heated by hot stones. A hunting party has returned towing a small whale. People will cut the whale fat into long strips and wear it around their necks, slicing off raw chunks of blubber once the feasting begins. There's a competition to see who can eat the most—the meat is swallowed whole because chewing is considered rude. The party could last all week!

A COASTAL VILLAGE

In the early 1800s, before European settlers arrived in the region, the Kwakwaka'wakw were still living in much the same way as they had for around 3,000 years. The ocean and the forests gave them more than they needed, so they lived in comfort despite their Stone Age technology. Each tribal group owned its own territory, living in permanent villages for most of the year but moving out to camps in the summer.

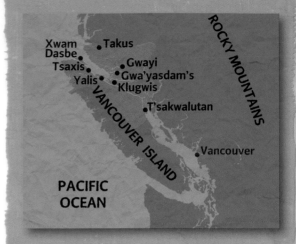

ROCKY MOUNTAINS

Xwam
Dasbe · Takus
Tsaxis · Gwayi
Yalis · Gwa'yasdam's
Klugwis
· T'sakwalutan

VANCOUVER ISLAND

· Vancouver

PACIFIC
OCEAN

THE NORTHWEST COAST

The Kwakwaka'wakw lived in a group of villages on Vancouver Island and on the adjoining mainland (area shaded in brown) northwest of what is now Vancouver, Canada. Although they were cut off from the rest of the continent by the Rocky Mountains, they had close links with other coastal peoples thanks to the Pacific Ocean, their highway.

Only senior tribal members could have big totem poles outside their homes

The houses were built from thick planks, which were cut from the giant cedar trees growing in the nearby forest

FAMILY FRIENDLY

Several families lived together in large wooden buildings known as longhouses. These had 20 ft (6 m) high ceilings but no windows, so it would have been dark inside except for the light from fires and the smoke hole in the roof. There was little furniture, but along one side of the longhouse was a wooden platform on which everyone slept. Every family had its own area, and the most important family lived behind a removable painted screen at the back of the longhouse.

Basket hats, made from tightly woven cedar roots, protected against the sun and rain

It took six months to weave a Chilkat blanket, which was worn by a tribal chief

Shoes were hardly ever worn, even in the snow

BENTWOOD BOX

The coastal peoples of western Canada were great woodworkers, weavers, and basket makers. This box was used for serving and storing food, especially during feasts. It was crafted from a single plank of cedar wood. The plank was steamed so it could be bent to form four sides. The box was held together with wooden pegs.

DUCK ROBES AND DOG WOOL

Due to the mild weather, the women simply wore short skirts and capes for most of the year, while the men wore breechcloths tucked into their belts (or nothing at all). These were made from cedar bark pounded into long, soft fibers and then woven. In very cold weather, bearskin coats were worn. Other robes were made from duck skins with the feathers still attached. Fluffy dogs were kept for their woolly coats, which were sheared like a sheep's.

The largest canoes were 60 ft (18 m) long and were built to handle storms and ocean currents

Food was cooked in cedarwood cooking boxes—stones were heated red-hot, then dropped into the box

The skills needed to make a canoe or totem pole were handed down from father to son

A totem pole was like a giant family history, with each animal or human carving telling a story

CANOE BUILDERS

A few men in every village were experts at building canoes. They split a cedar log in half, and shaped the outside using stones and sharp seashells. They made the inside hollow by burning it with controlled fire. Then they boiled water inside the canoe with hot rocks. This softened the wood, allowing the canoe builders to stretch and widen the sides with poles. Once dry, they carved, sanded (with rough dogfish skin), and painted the canoe.

PRESENTS FOR ALL

The coastal peoples celebrated events such as births, marriages, and deaths with a big party. Some lasted a fortnight, while smaller parties were held to give a chief back his dignity if he fell out of his canoe! They were called potlatches, from a local word meaning "to give away," since the host gave all the guests a gift. Visiting chiefs might be given slaves or canoes; others just received a woven basket or a copper bracelet.

Musical instruments were simple, such as this hide drum

A chief's house was painted with animals such as bears, eagles, and whales to show his importance

The chief and his family watched the dancers reenact ancestral stories

Dancers at the potlatch wore carved wooden masks— some had strings that were pulled to show different masks inside, like a magic trick

Fish was smoked over a small fire or hung up on the rafters of longhouses to dry

An old canoe was sometimes used to cook food in

Women helped to prepare, cook, and preserve the food

The sharp, pointed paddles could also be used as weapons

Sealskins blown up like balloons were used as floats and attached to fishing lines

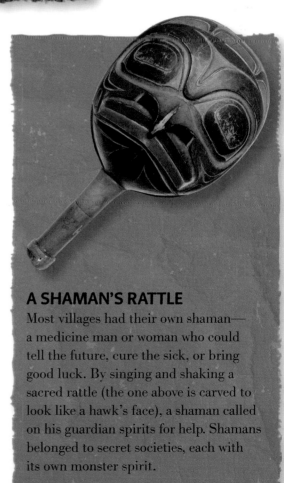

A SHAMAN'S RATTLE

Most villages had their own shaman— a medicine man or woman who could tell the future, cure the sick, or bring good luck. By singing and shaking a sacred rattle (the one above is carved to look like a hawk's face), a shaman called on his guardian spirits for help. Shamans belonged to secret societies, each with its own monster spirit.

WHAT'S FOR DINNER?

The coastal peoples didn't need to farm—they got all the food they needed from the sea and forest. Salmon was an important part of the diet, caught with hooks, nets, and spears. To keep it from rotting, the fish was smoked over a small fire. Giant halibut, seals, whales, and otters were hunted from canoes, while berries, seagulls' and puffins' eggs, seaweed, and shellfish were collected in woven baskets. Clams were dried and worn around the neck on a string, then eaten as a snack.

DIRTY OLD TOWN

At 4:30 AM, a watchman taps the window to wake the little girl and her family. After dressing, she chews on a hunk of bread as she walks toward the mill. The factory bell clangs, and she scampers in her shiny black clogs over the slippery cobblestones. Soon she is hard at work, cleaning the machines to keep them running smoothly. At noon, there is time for a bowl of soup before she is back at work, picking up the waste under the looms. The girl pinches herself. If she dozes off, the machines will chew her up. Finally, at 7:00 PM, she returns home, 14 hours after leaving.

In 1830s Britain, the pale faces and tired eyes of the mill workers tell their own story. Many are children, some of whom walk about 20 miles (30 km) a day around the factory as they move from loom to loom. No wonder they hobble around with swollen knees and ankles. Long working hours and a poor diet stunts their growth and weakens their resistance to disease. Amid the deafening roar of the machines, an eight-year-old is being scolded for dropping his can of oil. Although the Industrial Revolution has brought many changes, the poor are still poor. They are packed into rows of tiny houses strung along narrow streets. The air is thick with the sooty smoke that spews from the chimneys. There's sawdust in their bread and lead in their milk. The filthy water comes from a pump in the street. So why would anyone want to work here? New inventions such as threshing machines mean that many of the old farm jobs have vanished. Meanwhile, the big landlords have ringed the fields with fences and hedges, stopping ordinary people from grazing their animals or collecting firewood on what used to be common land. At least there's a steady job in the factory. There's no harvest to fail, so you won't starve.

A WORLD TRANSFORMED

By 1850, Britain had been transformed from a rural society in which most people lived and worked on the land, to one in which they lived and worked in cities. The changes, known as the Industrial Revolution, turned Britain into the wealthiest and most powerful country in the world. In time, the revolution spread to Germany, France, the United States, Japan, and Russia.

INDUSTRIAL BRITAIN

New towns based around the coal, steel, cotton, and shipping industries grew quickly as their populations exploded. Many were in the north and in the Midlands. Meanwhile, canals, and later railroad lines, crisscrossed the country, creating a network of industrial towns.

DAMP, DINGY, AND CRAMPED

The workers' houses were usually close to the factories so that people could walk to work. The houses were tiny, with a single room on each floor. They were often made of poor-quality bricks so the walls were constantly damp. There was little or no plumbing. Several families were crammed into one house, and the cramped and filthy living conditions led to the spread of diseases such as tuberculosis and cholera.

Laundry was done in tubs out in the streets, then hung on lines between the houses

The houses were built in back-to-back terraces around a communal toilet block and water pump

To clean the machines, children known as piecers crawled under the whirring machines—some were only four or five years old

WORK, WORK, WORK

Factories forced people to work in a different way. Hundreds of people were penned together under one roof, and the labor was boring and repetitive. Bullying overseers (supervisors) kept them hard at work, and the clocks were slyly put forward in the morning and back at night to lengthen the shifts. The only hope of rest was when the machines were turned off. By 1833, 84,000 mill workers in Britain were children. They were often killed or horribly injured in industrial accidents.

The air in the mills was thick with cotton dust, injuring workers' lungs

A weaving shed with hundreds of looms operating at the same time eventually made workers deaf

The children were often beaten by the factory overseers

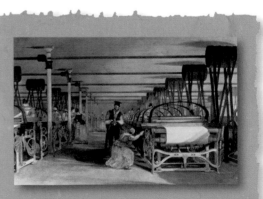

THE STEAM AGE

The invention of steam power led to a massive increase in the number of factories, especially textile mills. Steam engines revolutionized work. A single 100-horsepower engine had the strength of 880 men, could drive thousands of spindles at once, and could produce 60,000 miles (100,000 km) of thread in a 12-hour shift.

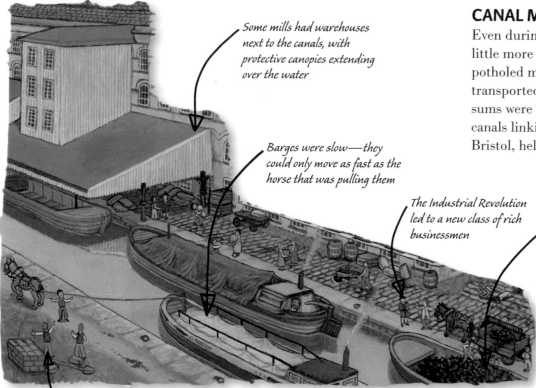

Some mills had warehouses next to the canals, with protective canopies extending over the water

Barges were slow—they could only move as fast as the horse that was pulling them

The Industrial Revolution led to a new class of rich businessmen

Canals and railroads were built by armies of workers known as "navvies," who had a reputation as troublemakers

CANAL MANIA

Even during the Industrial Revolution, most roads were little more than dirt tracks: bone-shakingly hard in summer, potholed mud baths in winter. Whenever possible, goods were transported on rivers or by sea. Between 1780 and 1830, huge sums were invested in a 4,000-mile (6,400 km) network of canals linking cities such as Birmingham, London, and Bristol, helping to create a transportation revolution.

Barges were perfect for transporting heavy goods such as coal and bricks, as well as fragile goods such as glass or china

Trains delivered letters and packages quickly around the country—the first postage stamp, the famous Penny Black, went on sale in 1840

THE IRON HORSE

By the 1830s, the canals had a serious rival—railroads. The construction of the Liverpool-Manchester line in 1830 proved that people and goods could travel faster than a speeding horse. Railroads made it cheap to bring raw materials to the factories and deliver finished goods and farm crops to the towns. People could also travel around the country easily and cheaply.

STEPHENSON'S ROCKET

The first steam trains were lumbering giants. In 1829, however, George and Robert Stephenson's *Rocket* (above) reached speeds of almost 30 mph (50 km/h), faster than a galloping horse. At first, people thought these speeds would damage their brains! Nine years later, the SS *Great Western*, designed by Isambard Kingdom Brunel, became the first paddle steamer built to carry passengers across the Atlantic Ocean. The world was getting smaller!

Chimneys, bridges, and factory smoke blocked out much of the light in industrial towns

TOXIC TOWNS

The growing towns were filthy and noisy, thanks to the railroads, the smoke from factory chimneys, and the soot from a thousand coal fires. This blackened the walls of houses and turned clothes gray in the rain. Carts, carriages, and horses clattered across cobblestones, adding to the noise. Work brought its own hazards. Workers in wallpaper factories were poisoned by the arsenic used in dyes, while small boys, used as chimney sweeps, often suffered burns or suffocated in chimneys.

1950s SUBURBIA

In 1950s America, wallets are bulging as the boom times are back! Out in the suburbs, every home has a backyard for the kids. Families work and play together and go on vacations to the new Disneyland in California. Cars rule, and freeways speed lines of traffic toward diners, bowling alleys, drive-in movie theaters, and shopping malls. Life is one big spending spree, and no home is complete without its own TV, refrigerator, and barbecue grill.

In the suburbs, row upon row of identical houses stretch into the distance, broken up by the occasional church steeple. Lawn mowers hum, a lone dog barks, and there's the whir of traffic in the distance. It's all very quiet and polite. On the weekends, men don aprons and chef's hats to barbecue steaks and pork ribs, while the women cook and chat in the kitchen. Outside, children catch Frisbees or shoot basketballs through hoops. Middle-class fathers wear gray flannel suits and their wives wear dresses with tight waists and high heels. Although people are very friendly, their world is closed to poor neighbors and African-Americans who have to fight to enjoy the same rights as others. But for all Americans, there is a real fear that the Soviet Union's nuclear weapons will blow them apart. Children practice safety drills at school and families build shelters in their backyard. However, there's plenty to distract young people from these worries. Ponytails, polka dots, and blue jeans are in, along with fast food. Teenagers twist to rock and roll and use slang such as "crazy" and "far out" to keep their parents in the dark, and sweethearts wear rings on chains around their necks to prove they are going steady.

THE AMERICAN DREAM

At the end of World War II, millions of young soldiers and sailors came back to the United States to pick up their lives and start new families and jobs. Throughout the war, magazines had advertised the "dream houses" being built in the suburbs, which had cheerful names such as Crystal Stream and Robin Meadows. As a result, many young couples headed out to the suburbs in search of the American Dream—a happy family life in a brand new home.

UNITED STATES

Detroit • • New York
Chicago • • Philadelphia
Los Angeles •
San Diego • • Memphis
Fort Worth • • Dallas
Houston • • New Orleans

The television, rather than the fireplace, became the focus of most living rooms

Many homes had their own refrigerators and other kitchen gadgets such as toasters and blenders

"Dream kitchens" were made from fitted, ready-made pieces that made them neat and easy to clean

Children enjoyed new toys such as Frisbees and Hula-Hoops

CHANGING AMERICA

During the 1800s, the United States was mostly a nation of farmers living in the country. From the 1880s onward, immigrants arrived in huge numbers from Europe. Cities such as New York, Chicago, New Orleans, and Detroit grew at a tremendous pace, some doubling in size every decade. In the 1950s, cities such as Los Angeles, Houston, Memphis, and Dallas spread out even farther thanks to the newly built suburbs.

FAMILY HOMES

During the 1950s, nine out of ten new houses in the suburbs were ranch houses. These were built on one floor to make them safer for young children. Most had a garage attached, a sliding glass door, and a patio for barbecues. The kitchen was at the front, so mothers could keep an eye on their children. The center of the home, the kitchen, had built-in cabinets and the latest electrical gadgets.

The jukebox was very popular—you put in a coin, selected a song, and the machine played the record

Often open all night, diners were a place for teenagers to meet after school or go on a date

RECORD PLAYER

In the 1950s, rock and roll was born with singers such as Bill Haley, Elvis Presley, and Chuck Berry ruling the airwaves. American teenagers also spent long hours listening to music on records—black vinyl disks that were played on portable record players (shown above). Horrified by the shaking hip movements of rock and roll, their parents preferred the gentle love songs of singers such as Nat King Cole and Frank Sinatra.

FAST FOOD

As Americans moved to the suburbs, they traveled farther to work. There was less time for sit-down dinners at the table. Families ate in shifts, often in front of the television. Workers wanted restaurants that offered food quickly, and ate their breakfast and lunch at cheap diners. As a result, people's eating habits changed. Fast food such as burgers, pizzas, and fried chicken became very popular, along with frozen food, ketchup, and soft drinks.

When the first African-American children were allowed into white-only high schools in 1957, they often faced angry protesters or were bullied at school

Dance crazes such as the hokey pokey, bunny hop, and hand jive swept the country

TELEVISION

By the end of the 1950s, most homes had a black-and-white television set. For the first time, people were eyewitnesses to important events such as wars. Before TV, children had no idea what most foreign countries looked like or how their peoples lived, and animals such as lions and giraffes were only names in books. Daytime programs such as soap operas helped advertisers sell products (especially soap) aimed at housewives.

TEEN REBELS

For the first time, teenagers were seen as a separate generation. Many wanted to be like movie star James Dean, who starred as a moody teenager in the film *Rebel Without a Cause* (1955) and made blue jeans a symbol of rebellion. They enjoyed watching TV shows such as Dick Clark's *American Bandstand* and reading teen magazines. Dancing to rock and roll was incredibly popular. Some high school students organized lunchtime dances, often in the school gym. These were called sock hops since dancers took their shoes off to avoid damaging the floor.

Greasers typically wore black leather jackets and always had their hair greased back

Most streets and roads now had concrete or asphalt surfaces, giving a smooth ride

Cars became lower, longer, and wider

Fins, wings, and afterburner tail lights made even family cars look like spaceships or jet fighters

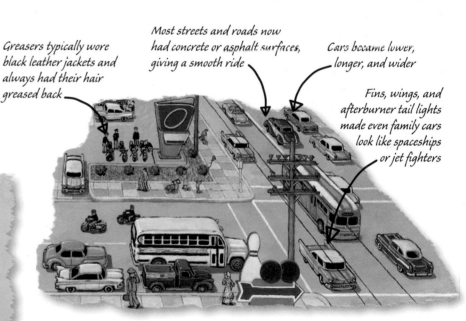

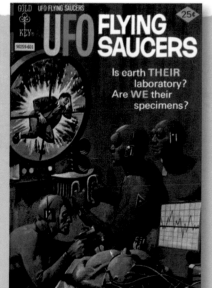

FLYING SAUCER

During the 1950s, people were worried that a nuclear war would break out between the Soviet Union and the United States. Such fears may be the reason why people across the country started seeing UFOs (unidentified flying objects): There were around 1,500 sightings in 1952 alone. Despite the lack of real proof, a spate of science-fiction movies appeared with scary names such as *The Thing* (1951) and *It Came From Outer Space* (1953).

ON THE ROAD

The sprawling suburbs were made possible by the automobile, which also led to the spread of diners, supermarkets, shopping malls, and drive-in movie theaters. Huge billboards lined the roadside. Cities were connected by a giant highway system. Gas was very cheap, and driving became something you did for fun: Teenagers went "cruising" around town with their friends or raced each other in "souped-up" (modified) cars, while gangs known as "greasers" raced around on motorcycles.

INDIAN BAZAAR

The bazaar is the heart of the city. Its streets and alleys pulse with people, traffic, and everyday life. Hawkers shout loudly at passersby to sample their wares. In the distance, there's the noise of the railroad line. A cyclist skilfully weaves through the traffic balancing a crate on his head, while an elephant and a cow amble along the middle of the road. On the sidewalk, a long line of schoolchildren holding hands threads a path. It's a very different world from the order and calm of the American suburbs, but somehow it all works!

Although it's the 1980s, some things haven't changed for centuries. The market opens at six in the morning and closes at nine in the evening. Vendors string marigolds and asters into garlands, hoping to catch the faithful on their way to the temple. A chai-wallah sells tea to tourists clustered around a snake charmer and his cobra. Nearby, a small boy yanks the leash before his monkey snatches a mango from the stall. Although the weather is hot and humid, a sari-clad teenage girl and her mother keep their cool as they haggle over silver bracelets. Motor rickshaws honk angrily as a truck refuses to budge. Oblivious to the noise, a holy man sits in silent meditation. Slowly but surely, however, India is changing. A skyscraper made of glass and steel soars into the sky. Electrical gadgets are sold next to silks and spices. On the radio, there's a report that India is blasting another satellite into space. The signs are already here that this ancient nation will transform itself into a global center for information technology and electronics within the next 30 years.

THE MELTING POT

During the 1980s, India was an ancient country in a modern world. Young women dressed in saris listened to American pop music and statues of goddesses marked with sacred ash sat on taxi dashboards. The country was a bewildering mix of religions, languages, and peoples, all living together in crowded cities swamped by a rapidly growing population.

Most Indians were part of a large extended family, so many generations often lived in the same house

INDIAN CITIES

India's mixed society is a result of a long history of invasion by Persians, Arabs, Mongols, Turks, and Muslim Mughals. By around 1800, Britain had gained control over most of the country, but in 1947, India became independent and the Muslim regions in the north were partitioned to form Pakistan and what later became Bangladesh. Its major cities were (and still are) Mumbai, Delhi, Kolkata, Chennai, and Bangalore.

LIFE-LONG COMMUNITY

From birth, most Indians are part of a jati, or community. There are more than 4,600 jatis, each linked to a particular job. Since ancient times the jatis have been arranged into four main groups, or castes: priests, warriors, traders, and servants. Even in the 1980s, those outside the caste system, known as the untouchables, were expected to do dirty jobs such as sweeping the streets or catching rats.

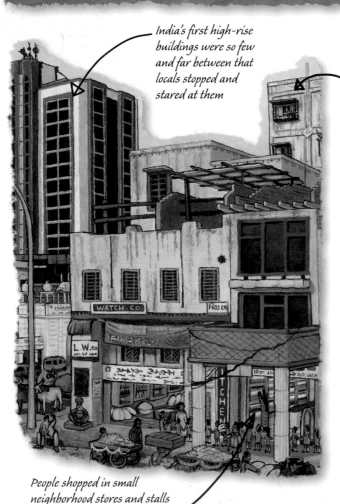

India's first high-rise buildings were so few and far between that locals stopped and stared at them

In this city of contrasts, ramshackle buildings housing the poor stood next to the skyscraper as the streets teemed with old and new forms of transportation

People shopped in small neighborhood stores and stalls rather than big supermarkets

UPS AND DOWNS

Today, tall skyscrapers crowd the skylines of Indian cities such as Mumbai. In the 1980s, however, there were very few high-rise buildings. While shopkeepers often lived above their stores, life was much harder for country people who came to the cities looking for work. They often lived in sprawling shantytowns on the edge of the city. Many people slept in the streets, especially near the railroad stations where workers were hired each morning.

AT THE MOVIES

Since the 1930s, India has produced hundreds of films every year, and for most Indians a trip to the movies is still a welcome escape from day-to-day life. The films are usually musicals with a mix of song-and-dance numbers, comedy, romance, and daredevil stunts. The catchy tunes are enjoyed by all ages, and can be heard blaring from stores, rickshaws, and homes.

On busy trains, many passengers hung out of the windows or even sat on the roof, risking life and limb

HOT AND CROWDED

A European visitor to Indian cities in the 1980s would have been struck by the heat and the very crowded streets. India's population had doubled in the previous 40 years, due to better medicine and a farming revolution in the 1960s. Unfortunately, many cities were overwhelmed by the flood of people from the country. The lack of housing, transportation, sewage, water, schools, and hospitals made life hard for many people.

TOURISM

The growth of the railroads and cheap travel in the 19th century encouraged tourism, and by the 20th century, millions of people around the world were going on vacation both at home and abroad. During the 1980s, India became popular with overseas tourists thanks to its rich culture and wonderful buildings and landscape. Popular destinations included the Taj Mahal in Agra (above). Completed around 1653, it was built by the Mughal emperor Shah Jahan in memory of his wife.

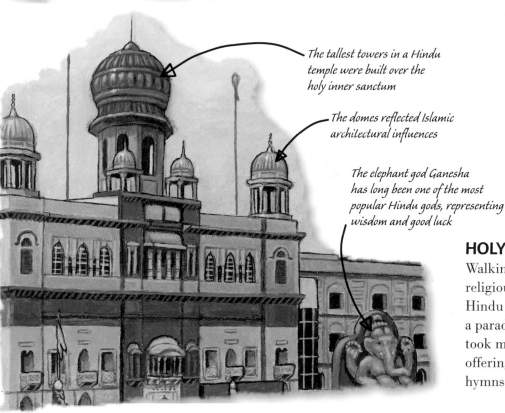

The tallest towers in a Hindu temple were built over the holy inner sanctum

The domes reflected Islamic architectural influences

The elephant god Ganesha has long been one of the most popular Hindu gods, representing wisdom and good luck

HOLY PLACE

Walking around city streets in the 1980s, you would see religious followers everywhere, from pilgrims visiting a Hindu temple, to Muslims offering prayers, to Sikhs holding a parade to celebrate a holy day. Religious rituals, or puja, took many forms: chanting, clapping hands, ringing bells, offering food, or meditation. Loudspeakers blasted out hymns or called the faithful to prayer.

ON THE MOVE

Around 80 years after the invention of the automobile, the city streets of India remained a throng of elephants, trucks, cars, rickshaws, and ox carts all mixed up, and some heading the wrong way down the road! Traveling on trains was just as chaotic, with every space taken up by passengers.

Some Indian temples had their own elephant; other elephants were decorated with paints and fabrics and used in ceremonies

Cows often wandered around city streets, adding to the traffic chaos

Rickshaws were a cheap way to get around and they could squeeze into the narrow lanes and alleys

Many carts and bicycles were piled high with goods or people

MODERN CITY

Downtown Tokyo is all about the future. Endless skyscrapers dominate the city, decked in flashing neon signs and two-story video screens plugging high-tech electronics, trendy clothes, and ingenious gadgets. As the sun sets, the city lights up in more ways than one. It's rush hour, and thousands of workers cram themselves onto bullet trains for the journey home. Others grab a quick bite from one of the fast-food stalls, or yatais. At a busy intersection, huge swarms of people cross the road every time a traffic light changes. Life is fast enough to make you dizzy!

Toyko is part of a supercity, or megalopolis, of more than 35 million people, and is one of the most crowded places on Earth. An ancient Shinto shrine, a designer shopping center, and a bustling food market are often just a quick walk apart. It's one big squash as commuters are shoved onto trains by pushers, cars are packed into multistory parking lots, and workers are crammed into small office spaces like sardines in a tin. Some workers stay at their desks long into the night, talking to clients in countries where it's time for lunch, and for those who have missed the last train home, there are tiny capsule hotel rooms for stopping overnight. The streets are heaving at all hours with shoppers, workers, and tourists. In addition to Japanese eateries such as noodle stalls, curry-rice shops, and sushi bars, you can find food from all over the planet. Thanks to modern communication and technology, the world has gotten a lot smaller. But global climate changes are making the world warmer, too. Parakeets and palm trees are increasingly common in Tokyo's concrete jungle. Making the most of the sun, many buildings have solar panels—some even have wind turbines—while recycling trucks do their part to help the planet. It's a very different world from the one cave dwellers inhabited!

69

LIFE IN THE FAST LANE

There are more than 34,000 people crammed into every square mile of Tokyo. As a result, skyscrapers are getting taller and giant indoor complexes are being built with offices, homes, and leisure facilities all under one roof. The city is also a wonderland of cutting-edge technology, from super-speedy bullet trains to robots that speak and move like humans.

Each room comes with its own TV, lighting, radio, and alarm clock

Busy workers spend the night in capsule hotels, sleeping in tiny rooms stacked side by side

NIGHT AND DAY

Japan has a reputation for being one of the hardest-working places in the world. Many people work long into the night or over the weekend. However, more and more people are working from home, too, helped by Japan's superfast broadband network and new technology such as video links.

Since Tokyo's streets are narrow, a maze of overpasses keeps the traffic moving, many two or three tiers high

Japan's bullet trains have reached speeds of more than 360 mph (580 km/h), whizzing commuters into work from the suburbs and from city to city

Today, most jobs require a knowledge of computers, whether for keeping track of money or goods, or for keeping in touch with clients

Since 1955, white-gloved oshiya (people pushers) have shoved passengers into already-packed trains

To speed up service and save space, customers in this fast-food restaurant pick up plates of sushi (seafood wrapped in rice) from a moving conveyer belt

FASTER AND FASTER

Every day, more than 10 million people commute into the center of Tokyo. This puts a huge strain on the transportation system. Just one station, Shinjuku, handles about 3.5 million passengers every day! Even so, most trains arrive within just a few seconds of their scheduled time, and huge crowds wait patiently for the next train. Although the groundbreaking bullet trains connect Tokyo to the country's other major cities, the trains are also used by commuters traveling to work from outlying areas.

Mexico City 20.7 million

New York 20.6 million

São Paulo 21.7 million

Delhi 28.6 million

Karachi 18.7 million

Mumbai 25.8 million

Dhaka 20.9 million

Kolkata 20.1 million

Tokyo 37.1 million

Shanghai 20.0 million

GLOBAL MEGACITIES

In 2008, for the first time in history, more than half of the world's population was living in towns and cities. This map shows the predicted size of megacities such as Tokyo, Mexico City, and Mumbai in 2025. But many smaller towns and cities are also growing fast.

Stalls sell street food such as octopus dumplings, pork buns, or a popular sponge cake known as castella

HUMANOIDS

When it comes to designing robots, Japan leads the world. For around 30 years, robots have been used in factories to build cars and other complex machinery. Some of today's models, however, look and behave just like humans. One of the latest, a female humanoid robot known as HRP-4C, has been designed to entertain people by singing and dancing. She is also programmed to show expressions such as anger or surprise.

STREET LIFE

Despite its size, Tokyo has been called a city of villages. Centered around a train stop or a large street, each part of the city has its own character. In between the gleaming skyscrapers, many buildings are just two or three stories high, separated by twisting lanes and alleys, or small squares with food markets open late into the night. Street musicians play for passersby, competing with the roar of traffic and music pumping from stores and car stereos.

Some new buildings have integrated wind turbines to help generate energy

ECO CITY

Many Japanese cities are affected by acid rain and smog, since the fumes created by factories and cars create air and water pollution. To counter these problems, Japan and many other countries are turning to renewable energy sources such as wind and solar power, and reducing pollution by recycling plastics and other products that are harmful to nature.

Many modern buildings use recyclable materials such as steel and plastic

Animated advertising screens bombard consumers with products you can now find anywhere in the world

MOBILE COMPUTERS

Computers have completely changed the way people work and play. The latest gadgets—smartphones and tablet PCs— allow people to do all kinds of tasks while on the move. A whole library of books, movies, and music can be stored inside, while the Internet allows the user to connect to the rest of the world.

GOING GLOBAL

In the 21st century, there are few places you can't get to in a day, and few areas you can't reach by phone. Even small businesses have customers or suppliers on the other side of the world. With international trade increasing by a factor of 100 in the last 50 years, more people are also traveling abroad to find work, while whole factories are often moved to another country where wages are lower.

Huge complexes house multiscreen movie theaters, ice-skating rinks, galleries, and offices, as well as a host of restaurants and stores

RIDDLES

Have you been looking closely? See if you can answer these riddles. The answers appear in the main scene for each period. Think about the puzzle, then take a look at the relevant pages. You can check the answers on page 80.

CAVE DWELLERS pages 8–9

I lie on the beach,
but I don't like the sun.
After a life in the water,
I'm a feast for someone.

I scare off animals,
but give a warm hello.
The longer I stand,
the shorter I grow.

EARLY FARMERS pages 12–13

I'm not a wolf,
but I sure can howl.
I'm a family's best friend,
when the big cats prowl.

Scooped from the river,
then squashed underfoot.
Dried by the sun,
once laid I stay put.

EGYPTIAN TEMPLE pages 16–17

I'm a pet for priests,
but my teeth can crush.
When it's written down,
my name sounds like "msh."

My beard is blue,
my hat is red.
I'm a towering stone giant,
now that I'm dead.

ROMAN TOWN pages 20–21

Although I'm a slave,
I've got lots of fans.
When I go to work,
there's blood in the sand.

I run from the hills,
straight as a spear.
What is my cargo?
It's transparently clear.

TEMPLE OF DEATH pages 24–25

Our view of the temple
is better than most.
If we fly too low
we'll soon be toast!

I make the gods happy,
but I'm feeling quite blue.
With a rope around your neck,
I'm sure you would too!

VIKING PORT pages 28–29

My head is a dragon,
but I don't breathe flames.
I float on the waves,
and long is my name.

A gift for the gods,
I'm all skin and bone.
I'm a welcome sight
outside a Norse home.

SPRING FESTIVAL pages 32–33

Flung from a boat,
day after day.
Like the web of a spider,
I snare my prey.

If you're being scared
by a spooky gang,
light my powder
and make me bang.

MEDIEVAL VILLAGE pages 36–37

My wheel keeps turning,
yet I'm stuck to the spot.
My life is a grind,
but that is my lot.

Armed with a bow,
I guard a farmer's plot.
But when I do my job,
I don't fire a single shot.

THE CAVEMAN

Imagine what it would be like to travel through history and see how much the world has changed through the ages. This is what the caveman has done. Here he is taking a look around on every spread. If you missed him, why not go back and see if you can track him down?

CITY OF GOLD pages 40–41

A ship of the desert,
without sails or mast.
No water for days,
I can drink at last.

Dark at the bottom,
sunny on top.
Light going down,
heavy coming up.

DIRTY OLD TOWN pages 56–57

I'm black when you get me.
I'm red when I'm used.
I'm gray when I'm finished.
Are you confused?

Perched on a hill
I'm terribly posh.
I look down on the workers
as they weave and wash.

SULTAN'S PALACE pages 44–45

One part of me bends,
the other part flies.
If I go where I'm sent,
somebody dies.

I'm covered in gold
and jewels that shine.
When my owner sits down,
the world stands in line.

1950s SUBURBIA pages 60–61

Shaped like a saucer,
I zip through the sky.
I go where I'm sent,
in the blink of an eye.

I'm a new breed of human,
neither adult nor child.
When I act up,
I get people riled.

TALE OF TWO CITIES pages 48–49

For most of the day,
I'm hidden from sight.
But I'm there just in case
nature calls in the night.

I bring the world closer,
whether earth, sea, or sky.
When the sun goes down,
I bring a twinkle to your eye.

INDIAN BAZAAR pages 64–65

Wrinkled, gray, and holy,
I'm as big as a truck.
If you leave behind an offering,
my statue brings good luck.

I have wings but no feathers,
a rudder but no sail,
a tail without fur,
and I'm as long as a whale.

PARTY BY THE SEA pages 52–53

Tall as a tree.
I'm full of glory.
Covered in faces,
I'm multistory.

I'm made from fine strands
woven into a frame.
I'm shaped like a cone
to keep off the rain.

MODERN CITY pages 68–69

I'm blown by the breeze.

I have windows but no doors,
and when I run I stay put.
Yet I can take you anywhere,
without moving a foot.

TIMELINE

Our world keeps on changing, sometimes in small steps, sometimes in giant leaps. Key events can shape our world, great thinkers can inspire new ways of being, while science and technology can transform the way we live. Take a look at this timeline to discover what happened before, during, and after our snapshots of history.

- c. 2.6 MILLION YEARS AGO (MYA) *Oldest tools crafted by early humans.*
- c. 1.5–0.5 MYA *Humans use fire.*
- c. 200,000 YA *First modern humans appear in Africa.*
- c. 200,000–28,000 YA *Neanderthals shared the modern world with humans.*
- c. 170,000 YA *Pinnacle Point is first inhabited by humans.*
- c. 70,000–14,000 YA *Humans leave Africa and spread across the world.*

- c. 9000 BCE *Animals, such as goats and sheep, bred in captivity.*
- c. 8700 BCE *First metalworking: objects made from copper.*
- c. 8000 BCE *Town of Jericho built. Cattle domesticated in western Asia.*
- c. 7500–5700 BCE *Çatal Hüyük flourishes.*
- c. 7000 BCE *By this time, wheat, barley, peas, and lentils grown in the Near East.*
- c. 6500 BCE *Cattle domesticated in north Africa.*

- c. 4000–3600 BCE *First wheeled vehicles invented.*
- c. 3200 BCE *Hieroglyphics written in Egypt.*
- c. 2700 BCE *First plumbing in Indus Valley civilization (now Pakistan).*
- c. 2550 BCE *Great Pyramid built in Egypt.*
- c. 1755 BCE *Law code of Babylonian King Hammurabi.*
- c. 1600 BCE *Canaanite people in western Asia invent the alphabet.*
- c. 1400 BCE *New Kingdom reaches its peak.*

- c. 520 BCE *Persian Empire at its greatest extent under Darius I.*
- 331 BCE *Alexander the Great conquers Persia.*
- c. 300 BCE *First aqueducts in Rome. By now, Celts have settled across much of Europe, including Britain.*
- 221 BCE *China united by first Qin emperor, Qin Shi Huang. Around this time, first printing in China using woodblocks on silk.*
- 30 BCE *Death of Cleopatra, last queen of ancient Egypt. Three years later, Augustus becomes the first Roman emperor.*
- c. 36 CE *Maya calendar in use.*
- c. 83 CE *Magnetic compass invented in China.*
- c. 117 CE *Roman Empire at its greatest extent under Emperor Trajan.*

PINNACLE POINT, SOUTH AFRICA, c. 160,000 YEARS AGO

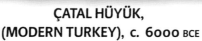

ÇATAL HÜYÜK, (MODERN TURKEY), c. 6000 BCE

ANCIENT EGYPTIAN TOWN, c. 1100 BCE

ANCIENT ROMAN TOWN, c. 130 CE

- c. 1500 *Songhai Empire expands.*
- 1519 *Leonardo da Vinci, Italian artist and inventor, dies.*
- 1519–22 *Ferdinand Magellan's expedition sails around the world.*
- 1519–33 *Spanish conquer Aztec and Inca empires.*
- 1530 *Beginning of African slave trade from west Africa to European colonies in the New World.*
- 1571 *Venetians defeat Ottomans at the Battle of Lepanto.*

- 1596 *Englishman John Harrington invents the flush toilet.*
- 1609 *Italian astronomer Galileo Galilei makes the first scientific observations of the moon and the planets using the newly invented telescope.*
- 1618–48 *Europe ravaged by 30 Years' War.*
- 1620 *From England, Pilgrims sail to America.*
- 1625 *Dutch establish a colony in North America named New Amsterdam (now New York).*

- c. 1700 *Age of Enlightenment in Europe.*
- 1712 *Englishman Thomas Newcomen invents the first commercially successful steam engine.*
- c. 1730–1840 *Industrial Revolution begins in Britain.*
- 1770 *British explorer James Cook lands in Australia.*
- 1776 *U.S. Declaration of Independence written.*
- 1783 *Montgolfier brothers build hot-air balloon in France. This is the first manned flight.*

- 1789 *Outbreak of French Revolution.*
- 1796 *English doctor Edward Jenner invents vaccine against smallpox.*
- 1800 *Italian scientist Alessandro Volta invents electric battery.*
- 1804 *Napoleon becomes French emperor.*
- 1805–6 *Scottish explorer Mungo Park explores Niger River. Americans Meriwether Lewis and William Clark cross the Rocky Mountains.*
- 1821 *British inventor Michael Faraday invents electric motor.*

TIMBUKTU, WEST AFRICA, c. 1500

TOPKAPI PALACE, ISTANBUL, c. 1600

AUSTRIAN CITY, c. 1730

SETTLEMENT, WEST COAST OF CANADA, c. 1800

- c. 320 *Rise of Gupta Empire in Ganges Valley, India.*
- 410 *Goths sack Rome. Beginning of Dark Ages in Europe.*
- 445 *Attila the Hun attacks Europe.*
- 476 *Fall of the Western Roman Empire.*
- c. 500 *Indian mathematical treatise (work), the Surya Siddhanta, determines the length of a year to within two seconds.*
- c. 575 *Indian mathematicians devise the decimal system of numerals (Arabic numerals) and the concept of zero.*
- c. 600 *Height of Maya civilization.*
- c. 634–712 *Muslim Arabs conquer much of Middle East, northern Africa, and Spain.*
- c. 789 *Vikings make their first raids on Britain.*

- c. 800 *First windmills built in eastern Persia (now Afghanistan).*
- 800 *Charlemagne becomes emperor of most of western Europe.*
- c. 820 *First use of paper money in China.*
- c. 850–900 *Gradual collapse of Maya civilization.*
- c. 900–1000 *Samurai warriors become important in Japanese warfare.*
- 871–99 *Alfred the Great rules England.*
- c. 900 *First castles built in western Europe.*
- 960–979 *Song Dynasty reunites China.*
- c. 1000 *Viking explorer Leif Ericsson lands in North America. Chinese use gunpowder in battle.*

- 1020 *First novel, Tale of Genji, written in Japan.*
- 1066 *Normans conquer England.*
- 1078 *William the Conqueror begins building the Tower of London, the first stone castle in England.*
- 1099 *Crusaders conquer Jerusalem.*
- 1187 *Turkish leader Saladin defeats crusaders and takes Jerusalem.*
- c. 1200 *Maori reach New Zealand.*
- 1206 *Mongol Empire founded by Genghis Khan.*
- c. 1237 *Spinning wheels used in Baghdad (in modern Iraq).*
- 1271 *Marco Polo sets out for China.*
- 1279 *Song Dynasty ends as Mongols crush Chinese forces.*
- 1299 *Ottoman dynasty founded in Turkey by Osman I.*

- c. 1300 *Huge stone statues erected on Easter Island in the Pacific Ocean.*
- 1324 *Emperor of Mali, Mansa Musa, goes on pilgrimage to Mecca.*
- 1347–9 *Black Death sweeps across Europe.*
- 1368 *Mongols driven out of China.*
- 1381 *Peasant's Revolt in England.*
- c. 1400 *Kingdom of Great Zimbabwe at its peak.*
- 1421 *Beijing becomes capital of Ming China.*
- c. 1438–1532 *Inca Empire at its peak.*
- c. 1455 *Gutenberg Bible printed using a movable-type printing press.*
- c. 1462–1520 *Aztec Empire at its peak.*
- 1492 *Christopher Columbus lands in America.*

MAYA TOWN, CENTRAL AMERICA, c. 700

VIKING TOWN, NORTHERN EUROPE, c. 900

SONG DYNASTY TOWN, CHINA, c. 1000

MEDIEVAL VILLAGE, FRANCE, c. 1400

- 1829 *George and Robert Stephenson build steam locomotive, Rocket.*
- 1833 *Britain abolishes slavery.*
- 1861–65 *Civil War and end of slavery in the United States.*
- 1863 *World's first underground railway system opens in London.*
- 1868–1912 *Meiji period sees industrial revolution in Japan.*
- 1873 *Levi Strauss manufactures blue jeans.*
- 1885 *German Karl Benz sells first motorcars.*

- 1908 *Production of the first affordable car—the Model T.*
- 1914–18 *World War I.*
- 1917 *Russian Revolution leads to creation of Soviet Union.*
- 1925 *In Britain, John Logie Baird gives the first public demonstration of the television.*
- 1928 *Alexander Fleming discovers the first antibiotic, penicillin.*
- 1939–45 *World War II.*
- c. 1955–68 *Campaign for civil rights in the United States.*

- 1961 *Yuri Gagarin becomes first man in space. Berlin Wall built.*
- 1969 *American astronauts land on the moon.*
- 1970–73 *First PCs developed*
- 1973 *First practical mobile phone developed in the United States.*
- 1976 *Launch of Apple I helps revolutionize home computing.*
- 1979 *Compact disc invented.*
- 1989 *Creation of the World Wide Web leads to the rapid growth of the Internet and e-mail.*

- 1989–91 *Berlin Wall comes down. Breakup of Soviet Union.*

MILL TOWN, BRITAIN, c. 1830

SUBURBAN TOWN, UNITED STATES, c. 1955

COSMOPOLITAN CITY, INDIA, c. 1980

TOKYO, JAPAN, TODAY

GLOSSARY

ABBEY
A Christian monastery or convent, headed by an abbot or abbess.

AMPHITHEATER
A large, oval stadium with tiers of seats. It was used by the ancient Romans for spectacles such as gladiator fights.

AQUEDUCT
A bridge that carries water over a valley. Most Roman cities were served by several aqueducts bringing water from lakes, rivers, and springs.

ARCHEOLOGIST
Someone who studies the past by looking at the remains of buildings and objects often buried under the ground.

BARBARIANS
The ancient Roman word for anyone who lived outside the empire, thought to be savages.

BAROQUE
A period from about 1600 to 1750 when the baroque style of art, architecture, and music flourished in Europe. Baroque art and architecture was often very ornate and grand.

BARRACKS
A building that houses soldiers, often found in forts and towns.

BCE
A method of dating. The abbreviation stands for "Before the Common Era," which covers the period of history before Jesus Christ was believed to have been born.

BILLBOARD
A large board used to advertise products, often found along busy roads.

BLADELETS
Tiny flakes of stone sharpened by Stone Age people and set in wood to make tools.

BLUBBER
A thick layer of fat under the skin of whales and other creatures.

BREECHCLOTH
A strip of material (usually a narrow rectangle) worn around the waist and tucked under a belt or string. Often worn by Native American men.

BREECHES
Pants ending above the knee and fastened with buckles, straps, or strings. Worn by many men in 17th- and 18th-century Europe.

CE
A method of dating, which stands for the "Common Era," the period after Jesus Christ was believed to have been born. Its first year is 1 CE.

COCKFIGHTING
A sport in which two roosters, trained to injure or kill each other, are placed in a small ring.

COURTIER
Someone who attends the court of a monarch or other powerful person. Often courtiers flattered a king or queen to get what they wanted.

DARK AGES
Troubled period of European history between the fifth and ninth centuries, marked by invasions and the decline of towns and cultural life.

DIVAN
The imperial council in the Ottoman Empire; also the name for a piece of Turkish furniture that looks like a couch.

DYNASTY
A line of rulers belonging to the same family. For example, members of the Song Dynasty ruled China from 960 to 1279 CE.

EMPIRE
A large area, with different peoples, under the rule of a single powerful state or people.

ENLIGHTENMENT
The movement in 18th-century Europe in which many thinkers put forward the idea that life's problems should be solved by science and reason rather than religion.

FALLOW
A field that isn't plowed or seeded for at least a year, allowing the soil to store up nutrients for the next growing season.

FLINT
A hard stone often used by Stone Age people to make tools. It was sharpened by chipping away flakes of stone with another rock.

FONTANGE
A towering hairstyle popular in the 18th century, named after the Marquise de Fontange, the mistress of King Louis XIV of France.

FOOT BINDING
The ancient Chinese custom of tightly wrapping the feet with bandages, inhibiting growth. It was practiced on girls, and was initially seen as a status symbol before becoming widespread. The custom was banned in 1911.

FORUM
A large open space in a Roman city. The forum was surrounded by public buildings, a temple, law courts, and expensive shops. It was also the center of commerce and town government.

FUNDUQ
The name for the inns once found in Arabic-speaking north and west Africa, used by travelers.

FYNBOS
Underground bulbs found only along the southern coast of South Africa, an important source of food for Stone Age peoples.

GLADIATOR
An armed fighter, usually a slave, who entertained ancient Roman audiences by fighting other gladiators or wild animals.

GLYPHS
Writing symbols often scratched into stone, such as those used by the ancient Maya.

GOTHIC
A style of architecture common in Europe between the 12th and 16th centuries and often used in medieval cathedrals. Typical elements include pointed arches and groups of tall columns.

GRAFFITI
Words scratched or painted onto walls, often with a rude or insolent message.

HAREM
The living quarters reserved for wives, female relatives, and mistresses in a Muslim household.

HARPOON
A spear with a barbed point used for hunting fish, whales, and other sea creatures.

HARROW
A large frame with several disks or teeth used by farmers to break up big lumps of soil after plowing. In medieval times, it was made of wood and pulled by horses or oxen.

HIERATIC
Ancient Egyptian writing used for everyday letters and documents, and written in ink.

HIEROGLYPHICS
An ancient Egyptian writing system using picture symbols, usually used for religious inscriptions and carved in stone.

ICE AGE
Cold periods in the past when huge glaciers covered a large part of the Earth's surface. The last Ice Age ended c. 9500 BCE.

JANISSARIES
Slave soldiers who were among the finest soliders in the Ottoman sultan's army.

JUNK
A Chinese sailboat common in medieval times and still in use today.

KNARR
A large merchant ship built by the Vikings.

LONGHOUSE
A long, narrow, single-room building built by various peoples in Europe and North America.

LONGSHIP
A Viking warship with oars and a square sail.

LOOM
A machine for weaving materials such as cotton or wool into cloth.

MANUSCRIPT
A book or document written by hand.

MIDDLE STONE AGE
Period of African prehistory from about 300,000 years ago to 50,000 years ago. At this time, most tools were made from stone, wood, or bone.

MINARET
A distinctive, tall tower found in most mosques. It is used for the call to prayer.

MINT
A building where coins are made.

MOSQUE
A Muslim place of worship.

MOVABLE TYPE
A printing system that uses pieces of wood or metal shaped into letters or characters. These can be moved around to form different words.

MUMMY
A dead body that has been preserved by freezing, drying, or adding chemicals.

NEW WORLD
North and South America, unknown to most Europeans until the voyage of Christopher Columbus in 1492.

NOMADS
People who have no permanent home but move around depending on the seasons.

OBSIDIAN
A type of black glassy rock produced by volcanoes, which can be shaped to make very sharp tools.

PADDLE STEAMER
A steam ship driven by large paddles at the back or sides.

PEDDLER
A traveling salesman.

PHARAOH
The ruler of ancient Egypt, both a king (or very rarely a queen) and a religious leader.

PILGRIMAGE
A long journey to a sacred or holy place.

POTLATCH
A feast held by peoples living on the northwestern coast of North America, in which the host handed out gifts to show off his wealth.

PYRAMID
A giant monument with a square base and four triangular sides, built by both the ancient Egyptians and the American peoples.

QURAN
The Muslim holy book.

RAMPART
A mound of earth or a wall built around a town.

REAPING
Cutting crops, usually during the harvest.

RUNES
A system of writing used by the Vikings.

SALON
A social gathering in the 18th century in which writers and artists met to discuss ideas.

SEDAN CHAIR
A cabin or chair with poles. Carried by porters, it allowed the rich to move around without getting dirty feet or being rained on.

SHADUF
A pole, used for raising water, with a bucket at one end and a weight at the other.

SICKLE
A tool for cutting crops, with a curved blade and a short handle.

SULTAN
A Muslim ruler.

THERMOPOLIA
Shops or bars selling cooked food in a Roman city.

TITHE
A tax paid to the church during medieval times, usually one-tenth of what you earned.

TOGA
A one-piece cloak worn by men in ancient Rome.

TOTEM POLE
A tall monument carved from trees and often decorated with animal sculptures that tell a story.

TREASURY
A room or building where gold, coins, and other precious objects can be stored safely.

VILLEIN
Medieval peasant farmer who paid rent to his lord in the form of goods and services.

WATTLE AND DAUB
A material used for building walls in medieval times. It consisted of rods and twigs woven together, then covered with mud or clay.

INDEX

CREDITS

The publisher would like to thank Carron Brown for the index.

The publisher would like to thank the following for their kind permission to reproduce their photographs:
(Key: a-above; b-below/bottom; c-center; f-far; l-left; r-right; t-top)

4 Alamy Images: Jerry Mason (crb). **5 Alamy Images**: PSL Images (tl). Getty Images: Yoshikazu Tsuno (bc). **11 Science Photo Library**: John Reader (tl, bl, cr). **14 Corbis**: Nathan Benn/Ottochrome (bl). **14–15 Corbis**: Nathan Benn/Ottochrome (Border). **15 Corbis**: Nathan Benn/Ottochrome (tl). **19 Corbis**: The Gallery Collection (c). **Getty Images**: De Agostini (tr). **23 Getty Images**: DeA Picture Library (tl); The Bridgeman Art Library (bl). **26–27 Dorling Kindersley**: CONACULTA-

INAH-MEX. Authorized reproduction by the Instituto Nacional de Antropología e Historia (tc/Border, bc/Border). **27 Corbis**: David Pillinger (bc). **Getty Images**: DeA Picture Library (cr). **30 Corbis**: Christophe Boisvieux (crb). **30–31 Corbis**: Mark Hannaford/JAI (Border). **31 Corbis**: Werner Forman (clb). **34–35 Corbis**: Pierre Colombel (Border). **35 Corbis**: Pierre Colombel (tr). **38 Getty Images**: French School (clb). **38–39 Corbis**: Peter Williams/Arcaid (Border). **39 akg-images**: (tl); British Library (crb). **42 TopFoto.co.uk**: The British Library/HIP (clb). **42–43 Corbis**: Walter Bibikow/JAI (Border). **43 Alamy Images**: blickwinkel (br); Wolfgang Kaehler (cra). **46–47 Corbis**: Brooklyn Museum (Border). **47 Alamy Images**: V&A Images (tr). **Getty Images**: Turkish School (bc). **50–51 Corbis**: The Art Archive (Border). **51 Alamy Images**: Lebrecht Music

and Arts Photo Library (tc). **TopFoto.co.uk**: IMAGNO/Austrian Archives (AA) (cr). **54 Corbis**: Canadian Museum of Civilization (bl). **54–55 Dorling Kindersley**: Hubbell Trading Post National Historic Site, Arizona (Border). **55 Dorling Kindersley**: The American Museum of Natural History (crb). **58 Getty Images**: Thomas Allom (crb). **58–59 Dorling Kindersley**: Science Museum, London (Border). **59 Getty Images**: SSPL (clb). **62 Corbis**: Lawrence Manning (cb). **62–63 Getty Images**: Steve Taylor (Border). **63 The Advertising Archives**: (bl). **Corbis**: Bettmann (tr). **67 The Kobal Collection**: BR Films/United Producers (crb). **70–71 Corbis**: Jose Fuste Raga (Border).

All other images © Dorling Kindersley
For further information see: www.dkimages.com

RIDDLE ANSWERS

CAVE DWELLERS

I'm the beached whale that appears on page 9. I could easily feed a large tribe!

I'm the fire burning on page 8. Without me, Stone Age peoples would not have been able to cook, heat themselves, or keep their caves lit.

EARLY FARMERS

I'm one of the dogs on page 13. I was more vicious than today's pets, and I made a useful guard against attacks by wild animals.

I'm a mud brick used by early peoples to build their houses. You can see me being made at the bottom of page 12.

EGYPTIAN TEMPLE

I'm the crocodile on page 16. In ancient Egyptian writing I represented the sound "msh." I was often kept as a sacred pet in some temples, where the priests fed me fine meats and wine, and dressed me in gold earrings and bracelets!

I'm one of the giant statues of former pharaohs that stand guard outside the entrance to the temple, a common practice in ancient Egypt.

ROMAN TOWN

I'm a gladiator. You can see me being mobbed by fans on page 20. The word *arena* means sand in Latin, since sand was sprinkled onto the floor to soak up the blood of wounded or dead gladiators.

I'm the big aqueduct that you can see in the background on page 21. I supplied every Roman city with fresh water for drinking, baths, and fountains.

TEMPLE OF DEATH

We're the two macaws flying over the temple on page 24. The Mayans hunted us for food as well as for our feathers, which they used to make headdresses.

I'm one of the captives waiting to be sacrificed to the Maya gods on top of the temple. The famous Maya blue used to paint me was made from plant dyes mixed with clay.

VIKING PORT

I'm the longship on page 28. The dragon head on my prow was put there to terrify the enemy.

I'm the horse sacrifice outside the house in the middle of page 28. Sacrifices were made for three festivals: one in autumn so there would be plenty of food to eat in winter, one in winter so the crops would grow well in spring, and one in spring to ensure successful raids and expeditions during the summer.

SPRING FESTIVAL

I'm the fishing net being thrown on page 32. When I was no longer needed, I was sometimes mixed with mashed bark to make paper.

I'm the bamboo firecracker being lit on page 33. The Chinese used me to scare away evil spirits, especially one called Nian who looked like a unicorn.

MEDIEVAL VILLAGE

I'm the water mill on page 36. The ancient Greeks invented me in the third century BCE.

I'm the scarecrow at the bottom of page 37. In medieval times, I was often given a bow and arrow to make me look scarier.

CITY OF GOLD

I'm one of the camels on page 41. I walk with a rocking motion that can make some riders seasick. It's not the only reason I'm called a ship of the desert—there's no better animal for carrying a heavy load across the desert since I can go without water for 10 days or more!

I'm the well at the bottom of page 41. A well like me may have given Timbuktu its name: *Tim* means "well" in the Berber language, while *Buktu* refers to a small sand dune.

SULTAN'S PALACE

I'm the bow and arrow being mounted by archers on page 44. Made from a mix of horn, wood, and sinew (animal fibers), Ottoman bows like me were known for their great power and beautiful design.

I'm the gold-plated sultan's throne on page 45. When the sultan went to war, I went too!

TALE OF TWO CITIES

I'm the blue chamber pot sitting on the floor (behind a screen) on page 48. Once used, my contents were thrown out into the streets!

I'm the telescope being used in the attic on page 49. I was invented in Holland in 1608, and a year later the famous Italian astronomer Galileo Galilei used me to study the Moon and the planets.

PARTY BY THE SEA

I'm one of the tall totem poles on pages 52 and 53. I describe the important people and events in a family's past. Over the ages, other peoples in Korea, Japan, and New Zealand built similar wooden poles or pillars decorated with carvings of animals.

I'm one of the basket hats you can see on page 53. I was made from finely woven spruce roots or cedar bark. My design and pattern showed a person's importance and family connections.

DIRTY OLD TOWN

I'm the coal in the barge on page 56. In the 1830s, I was still being dug from the ground by children in English coal mines. It was dark, dirty, and often lonely work.

I'm the mansion you can see on top of the hill on page 56. I was a stately home for the owner of the mill, a symbol of his wealth and power. I was much bigger and more comfortable than the tiny, dirty homes his workers lived in.

1950s SUBURBIA

I'm the frisbee being thrown on page 60. The idea first came from American college students in the 1940s. They discovered that pie tins were great for playing catch! So, in the 1950s, I was made from plastic and called the Pluto Platter.

I'm one of the teenagers on pages 60 and 61. Before the 1930s, most teenagers like us left school and started work at a young age. But in the 1930s, President Roosevelt set up a program that enabled us to stay in high school. Now there was more time for music, dancing, or just hanging out!

INDIAN BAZAAR

I'm the statue of Ganesha, the elephant god, on page 64. I am an important Hindu god, and I am known for my knowledge and for bringing good luck.

I'm the passenger jet flying across the sky on page 65. The first airliner to have jet engines like me, the *Comet*, flew from London, England, to Johannesburg, South Africa, in 1952.

MODERN CITY

I'm the wind turbine on the rooftop on page 68. As the world's resources of oil and gas run out, more and more cities will rely on alternative energy sources like me, as well as solar panels and biogas.

I'm one of the computers you can see in the office on page 69. Thanks to the Internet, computers can now connect people to the rest of the world at the click of a button. On my screen you will find your way around using my "windows," and I run on electricity, not legs!